Hold on to Your FORK!

(And fifty-one additional inspiring stories from the Internet for those who do not use a computer)

Compiled By

GLEN WHEELER, D.D

Koinonia Associates
Knoxville, Tennessee

ISBN 978-1-60658-026-4

Published by:
Koinonia Associates
7809 Timber Glow Trail
Knoxville, TN 37938

To learn how you can become a published author, visit
PublishwithKA.com
November 16, 2012

Cover Artist: Sarah Wells, Columbus, OH
Editor: Kathy Termeer, Columbus, OH

The inspiration for this book.
EVELYN RUTH WHEELER
1925-1981

ABOUT THIS BOOK

"Go to the Web, Facebook, or Twitter" the church bulletin, the sports announcers, the advertisers, and the news reporters advise. However, to most of the population over sixty, these are useless instructions, for most Senior Citizens do not own a computer. They do not get the "rest of the story." Health, limited eyesight, deafness, and memory loss prevent the use of a computer. Handicapped, aging, confinement to a wheelchair or bed are other hindrances.

However, there are many inspiring articles which would lift their spirits if they could hear or read them. This book was primarily compiled for those without a computer or unable to use one, but, the articles are worth reading by any one of any age.

For twelve years, I served as Chaplain at the Worthington Christian Village, Columbus, OH. There was a computer room for the residents . Many desired to learn how to email their children and grandchildren. They were disappointed when the frailties of age hindered their mastering the necessary skills.

For years I have been an avid collector of material for sermons and other types of speeches. Inspiring articles are abundant. The selection in this book are uplifting, humorous, and challenging. Keep a box of Kleenex nearby.

Many people have a ministry of reading to the blind and those of limited abilities, to residents of retirement and nursing homes, and to those with long term illnesses. This book will be a blessing. It would make a good birthday, special occasion or Christmas gift.

May I be so bold as to invite responses as to how these stories were used or responses to them? Additional books could be published if they fill a need. My address is in the back of the book.

Being a Senior Citizen, and with memories from many years of ministry, I have chosen these stories to strengthen, bless and comfort my generation.

May God bless you and those with whom you share this book.

Glen Wheeler, Compiler

IN GRATITUDE

To Judie, David and Dennis who have honored Evelyn Grove Wheeler with their love and lives.

To the congregations of the Christian Churches in Morristown and Harriman, TN, West Frankfort, IL, Ironton, OH, and North East, Columbus, OH, who graciously permitted me to serve as minister and heard many of these stories.

To Kathy Termeer for her skills in editing the manuscript.

To artist Sarah Wells for her cover design.

To the staff at Koinonia Associates for their valuable assistance.

To the Administration, Staff, Volunteers and Residents of the Worthington Christian Village, Columbus, OH for their friendship through the many years of my residency at the village.

To all who have touched my life and family during the more than sixty-five years of ministry and helped to make it, "A Wonderful Journey."

THANK YOU!

AUTHORSHIP

I do not claim authorship of any article in this book except for chapter one. When articles appear on the computer, authorship is rarely mentioned. I have included the name of the author if given.

Please advise me of any errors and correction will be made in future editions.

Table of Contents

Hold onto Your Fork

By GLEN WHEELER

In Robert Browning's poem, "Rabbi Ben Ezra," this phrase is found: "Grow old along with me, the best is yet to be. . . ." Since 1963, my wife Evelyn and I frequently quoted this phrase to each other. It was a mutual expression of encouragement, that bolstered us through many difficult times.

During the past year, another little phrase became a part of my life and it has been as helpful as the first. This second phrase is simply, "Hold on to your fork."

It was over a cup of coffee that a friend told me about a preacher named Carl Hicks, who spoke to his civic club one day and used this topic, "Hold on to Your Fork" meaning—hold on to your Faith regardless what comes your way. These words were just what I needed and how they have meant so much to me!

Just a few weeks before, Evelyn had passed away and I was still grieving. Even though she had suffered from ill health most of her life and for the past seventeen years had been kept alive by a Starr-Edwards artificial heart valve, I was still heartbroken. Even though in my ministry I had ministered to hundreds of others in their sorrow, I was in need of ministry. This phrase, "Hold on to your fork," spoke directly to my needs.

I developed this phrase into an illustration that I have used in speaking to others on this topic. It has been suggested that it be shared via the printed page. I trust you will find it helpful.

A story – Recall in your mind the most delicious meal you have ever enjoyed. It could have been in your home, at a restaurant, or at a family get-together. It could have been at a church meeting, a cook-out, or on a special occasion. But let your mind go back to that memorable time.

Do you recall that as the meal came near an end, the host or hostess would urge you to have additional meat, more vegetables or salad? Your response was, "Thank you, but I am so full, I cannot eat another bite." This dialogue would be repeated two or three times until at last, the hostess would begin removing the dinner plates from the table. As each plate was removed, she would say, "Hold on to your fork." Why would she say that when you had already stated there was no room for any more food? Because she knew what was coming – and that it would be the best part of the meal.

In a few moments, the hostess returned with a generous helping of your favorite dessert. Immediately, forgetting your previous comments, you picked up the fork and enjoyed the best part of the meal. No wonder she said, "Hold on to your fork!" And this is the way life is.

A life - Remember high school days, when life was a song? The class plays, the sports activities, the National Honor Society, the dates, the yearbooks, etc. Then, when graduation came, the walk across the stage for your diploma and the movement of the tassel on your hat? I still remember my 1943 graduation from Lincoln High School, Vincennes, Indiana. I thought I was the greatest. About the time the tassel was moved, the message, "Hold on to your fork" was whispered.

And sure enough, the opening of the next school term found me in the enrollment line and my college adventure began. High school days were soon forgotten as college life unfolded. I recall the fall of 1943 when I enrolled at Johnson Bible College, Knoxville, Tenn., and many of the emotions I had.

Four-hundred miles away from home, among strangers, sharing a dorm room – the changes seemed endless. But, finally at the end of four years, there came the thrilling graduation night. Again, I walked across the platform, received my diploma, moved the tassel, and seemed to hear again, "Hold on to your fork."

And so I did – for on August 31, 1948, the strains of Lohengrin's wedding march filled the sanctuary of the First Christian Church, Vincennes, Ind. I thrilled as I watched a beautiful bride walk toward me, escorted by her father. The minister, Dr. Ray H. Montgomery, Sr., listened as Evelyn and I pledged those familiar words. Little did we know how prophetic they were. We took each other, "for better, for worse; for richer, for poorer, in sickness and in health, to love and to cherish until death parts us." Was I ever happy I had held on to my fork!

All that I ever dreamed about having was now ours. A ministry at First Christian Church, Harriman, Tenn., our first car, our own home, our own bank account, our first mortgage, our first credit card. What more could we ask? But that haunting refrain came once again, "Hold on to your fork." What could be better?

In few years, here came a little boy to bless our home and a few years later, another one. You know how new fathers act. Even though I was a preacher, I was no different in bragging about the children.

After eight years in Harriman, we moved to West Frankfort, Ill. While there, Evelyn's fragile health caused her to suffer her first heart attack and we were confronted with the fact she would not live a normal life span. We faced many questions and uncertainties, but the rewards of faith are so many.

When we moved to Ironton, Ohio in 1961, we had no idea of the adventure before us or how many times we would assure each other that the best was yet to be.

In 1963, the local doctors referred Evelyn to the Cleveland (Ohio) Clinic where, after a series of tests and evaluations, they advised and performed open-heart surgery. A metal heart valve was implanted. She was one of the early pioneers in this type of heart surgery.

The doctors advised us that she might live three to five years. So, we tried to live each day to the fullest and make as many priceless memories as possible. A young lady of our church took as her ministry, the care of the preacher's wife and she became a part of the family. At Christmas time, Evelyn gave me a watch chain, with a miniature heart valve and a charm which read, "Stick with me, the best is yet to be."

The next few years passed. Then five years passed, then ten and twelve and fifteen –far longer than the doctors had anticipated. We had our highs and lows, our mountaintops and our valleys. Our children married and three granddaughters blessed us.

Evelyn's ministry literally reached hundreds who, in life's situations sought strength, advice and comfort from one who had walked in their shoes so many years. Her courage and infectious laughter were ever present and practiced, along with her deep and radiating and unwavering faith.

Then the fork seemed to waver when in 1977, while attending the North American Christian Convention in Cincinnati, she lost her eyesight in the span of forty-eight hours, as a result of an embolism. Only 20 percent of her sight returned. The following three years were years of great adjustments.

The Northeast Church of Christ, Columbus, OH. extended us a call in the fall of 1978, and the facilities of the University Hospital were available to us.

In December of 1980, the doctors advised that complications were present in her heart and they felt that the heart valve, which had now been in place for over seventeen years should be replaced and that the aorta valve needed to have an artificial one implanted.

On March 1, 1981, she entered the hospital for the surgery. This was performed on March 3. Early in the morning of March 5, the doctors brought the news we dreaded to hear, "We're sorry, but we did all we could." And the fork not only slipped, but it seemed to break. After so many years, it just did not seem possible that this beautiful one was gone.

We did what every other family does in like situations. The final arrangements were made and services were held at the Northeast Church of Christ, Columbus, OH.

We then held the services of praise, victory, thanksgiving and love at the beautiful Central Christian Church, Ironton, where she had ministered with me for more than fifteen years. It was an inspiring tribute to her life and influence.

A lesson – Then came the pilgrimage to the peaceful Woodland Cemetery. But this time, I was in the family car behind the hearse, instead of in the preacher's car in front of the hearse. What a change in view this is.

After the graveside services, I lovingly touched her casket, then reluctantly got into the family car to leave. As my brother started to pull away, I did what I have seen hundreds of other family members do when I had conducted services for their loved ones. As the car pulled away, I slightly turned for one final glimpse of the flower covered mound.

Even though my eyes were filled with tears and my heart seemed to be nearly bursting, it seemed as if I heard a familiar feminine voice whisper, "Glen, hold onto you fork. The best is yet to be. . . it really is! I know."

Glen Wheeler is a retired minister, living at the Worthington Christian Village, Columbus, OH.

Reprinted by permission of Standard Publishing, Cincinnati, Ohio 45231. From CHRISTIAN STANDARD, May 23, 1982, pages 12 ,13.

A Blind Man's Wedding

A remarkable incident occurred at a wedding in England. A young man, William Montagu Dyke, of large wealth and high social position, who had been blinded by an accident when he was ten years old, and who won university honors in spite of his blindness, had courted and won a beautiful bride, although he had never looked upon her face.

A little while before his marriage he submitted himself to a course of treatment for his eyes by experts. The climax came on the day of his wedding. The day came, and the presents, and the guests. There were cabinet ministers and generals and bishops and learned men and a large number of fashionable men and women. William Montagu Dyke, dressed for his wedding, his eyes still shrouded in linen, was driven to the church by his father, and the eye doctor met them in the foyer.

The bride, Miss Cave, entered the building on the arm of her white-haired father, the admiral, who was all decked out in blue and gold lace. So moved was she that she could hardly speak. Was her beloved at last to see her face–the face that others admired, but which he knew only through his delicate fingertips?

As she neared the altar, while the soft strains of the Wedding March floated through the church, her eyes fell on a strange group. Sir William Hart Dyke stood there with his son. Before the latter was the eye doctor in the act of cutting away the last bandage.

William Montagu Dyke took a step forward, with the spasmodic uncertainty of one who can not believe that he is awake. A beam of rose-colored light from a pane in the church window fell across his face, but he did not seem to see it. Did he see anything? Yes! Recovering in an instant his steadiness of countenance, and with a dignity and joy never before seen in his face, he went forward to meet his bride. They looked into each other's eyes, and one would have thought that his eyes would never wander from her face."At last!" she said. "At last!" he echoed solemnly, bowing his head.

A Date with the Other Woman

After 21 years of marriage, I discovered a new way of keeping alive the spark of love. A little while ago I started to go out with another woman. It was really my wife's idea.

"I know you love her," she said one day, taking me by surprise.

"But I love YOU!" I protested.

"I know, but you also love her."

The other woman my wife wanted me to visit was my mother, who has been a widow for 19 years. The demands of my work and my three children had made it possible to visit her only occasionally.

That night, I called to invite her to go out for dinner and a movie.

"What's wrong, are you well," she asked? My mother is the type of woman who suspects that a late night call or a surprise invitation is a sign of bad news.

"I thought it would be pleasant to pass some time with you," I responded. "Just the two of us."

She thought about it for a moment, then said, "I would like that very much."

That Friday, after work, as I drove over to pick her up I was a bit nervous. When I arrived at her house, I noticed that she, too, seemed to be nervous about our date. She waited in the doorway with her coat on. She had curled her hair and was wearing the dress that she had worn to celebrate her last wedding anniversary. She smiled from a face that was as radiant as an angel's.

"I told my friends that I was going to go out with my son, and they were impressed," she said, as she got into the car. "They can't wait to hear about our evening."

We went to a restaurant that, although not elegant, was very nice and cozy. My mother took my arm as if she were the First Lady.

After we sat down, I had to read the menu. Her eyes could only read large print. Halfway through the entree, I lifted my eyes and saw Mom sitting there staring at me. A nostalgic smile was on her lips.

"It was I who used to have to read the menu when you were small," she said. "Then it's time you relaxed and let me return the favor," I responded.

During the dinner, we had an agreeable conversation - nothing extraordinary- just catching up on recent events of each other's lives. We

14

talked so much that we missed the movie.

As we arrived at her house later, she said, "I'll go out with you again, but only if you let me invite you." I agreed and kissed her good night.

"How was your dinner date?" asked my wife when I got home. "Very nice. Much nicer than I could have imagined," I answered.

A Dreamer and His Dream

Let me tell you, Jesse hated this job and you would too, I imagine, if you had to do it. Jesse was a chicken plucker. That's right.

He stood on a line in a chicken factory and spent his days pulling the feathers off dead chickens so the rest of us wouldn't have to.

It wasn't much of a job. But at the time, Jesse didn't think he was much of a person. His father was a brute of a man. His dad was actually thought to be mentally ill and treated Jesse rough all of his life.

Jesse's older brother wasn't much better. He was always picking on Jesse and beating him up. Yes, Jesse grew up in a very rough home in West Virginia.

Life was anything but easy. And he thought life didn't hold much hope for him. That's why he was standing in this chicken line, doing a job that very few people wanted.

In addition to all the rough treatment at home, it seems that Jesse was always sick. Sometimes it was real physical illness, but way too often it was all in his head. He was a small child, skinny and meek. That sure didn't help the situation any.

When he started to school, he was the object of every bully on the playground. He was a hypochondriac of the first order.

For Jesse, tomorrow was not always something to be looked forward to. But, he had dreams. He wanted to be a ventriloquist. He found books on ventriloquism. He practiced with sock puppets and saved his hard earned dollars until he could get a real ventriloquist dummy.

When he got old enough, he joined the military. And even though many of his hypochondriac symptoms persisted, the military did recognize his talents and put him in the entertainment corp.

That was when his world changed. He gained confidence. He found that he had a talent for making people laugh, and laugh so hard they often had tears in their eyes. Yes, little Jesse had found himself.

You know, folks, the history books are full of people who overcame a handicap to go on and make a success of themselves, but Jesse is one of the few I know of who didn't overcome it. Instead he used his paranoia to make a million dollars, and become one of the best-loved characters of all time in doing it!

Yes, that little paranoid hypochondriac, who transferred his nervousness into a successful career, still holds the record for the most

Emmy's given in a single category.

The wonderful, gifted, talented, and nervous comedian who brought us Barney Fife was Jesse Don Knotts. NOW YOU KNOW,"THE REST OF THE STORY".

A Fifty-Seven Cent Church

A little girl stood near a small church from which she had been turned away because it was 'too crowded. ' 'I can't go to Sunday School,' she sobbed to the pastor as he walked by.

Seeing her shabby, unkempt appearance, the pastor guessed the reason and, taking her by the hand, took her inside and found a place for her in the Sunday school class. The child was so happy that they found room for her, and she went to bed that night thinking of the children who have no place to worship Jesus.

Some two years later, this child lay dead in one of the poor tenement buildings. Her parents called for the kindhearted pastor who had befriended their daughter to handle the final arrangements.

As her poor little body was being moved, a worn and crumpled red purse was found which seemed to have been rummaged from some trash dump. Inside was found 57 cents and a note, scribbled in childish handwriting, which read: 'This is to help build the little church bigger so more children can go to Sunday School.'

For two years she had saved for this offering of love.

When the pastor tearfully read that note, he knew instantly what he would do. Carrying this note and the cracked, red pocketbook to the pulpit, he told the story of her unselfish love and devotion.

He challenged his deacons to get busy and raise enough money for the larger building.

But the story does not end there.

A newspaper learned of the story and published it. It was read by a wealthy realtor who offered them a parcel of land worth many thousands. When told that the church could not pay so much, he offered to sell it to the little church for 57 cents.

Church members made large donations. Checks came from far and wide. Within five years the little girl's gift had increased to $250,000.00–a huge sum for that time (near the turn of the century). Her unselfish love had paid large dividends.

When you are in the city of Philadelphia, look up Temple Baptist Church, with a seating capacity of 3,300. And be sure to visit Temple University, where thousands of students are educated.

Have a look, too, at the Good Samaritan Hospital and at a Sunday School building which houses hundreds of beautiful children, built so that no child in the area will ever need to be left outside during Sunday school time.

In one of the rooms of this building may be seen the picture of the sweet face of the little girl whose 57 cents, so sacrificially saved, made such remarkable history. Alongside of it is a portrait of her kind pastor, Dr. Russell H. Conwell, author of the book, *Acres of Diamonds*.

This is a true story, which goes to show WHAT GOD CAN DO WITH 57 CENTS.

A Pillow and a Blanket

A long time ago, a young, wealthy girl was getting ready for bed. She was saying her prayers when she heard a muffled crying coming through her window. A little frightened, she went over to the window and leaned out.

Another girl, who seemed to be about her age and homeless was standing in the alley by the rich girl's house. Her heart went out to the homeless girl, for it was the dead of winter, and the girl had no blanket, only old newspapers someone had thrown out.

The rich girl was suddenly struck with a brilliant idea. She called to the other girl and said, "You there, come to my front door, please." The homeless girl was so startled she could only manage to nod.

As quick as her legs could take her, the young girl ran down the hall to her mother's closet, and picked out an old quilt and a beat up pillow. She had to walk slower down to the front door as to not trip over the quilt which was hanging down, but she made it eventually.

Dropping both the articles, she opened the door. Standing there was the homeless girl, looking quite scared. The rich girl smiled warmly and handed both articles to the other girl. Her smile grew wider as she watched the true amazement and happiness alight upon the other girl's face. She went to bed incredibly satisfied.

In mid-morning the next day a knock came to the door. The rich girl flew to the door hoping that it was the other little girl there. She opened the large door and looked outside. It was the other little girl. Her face looked happy, and she smiled. "I suppose you want these back."

The rich little girl opened her mouth to say that she could keep them when another idea popped into her head. "Yes, I want them back."

The homeless girl's face fell. This was obviously not the answer she had hoped for. She reluctantly laid down the beat up things, and turned to leave when the rich girl yelled, "Wait! Stay right there."

She turned in time to see the rich girl running up the stairs and down a long corridor. Deciding whatever the rich little girl was doing wasn't worth waiting for she started to turn around and walk away.

As her foot hit the first step, she felt someone tap her on the shoulder, turning she saw the rich little girl, thrusting a new blanket and pillow at her. "Have these." she said quietly.

These were her own personal belongings made of silk and down feathers.

As the two grew older they didn't see each other much, but they were never far from each other's minds. One day, the Rich girl, who was now a rich woman got a telephone call from someone, a lawyer, saying that she was requested to see him.

When she arrived at the office, he told her what had happened. Forty years ago, when she was nine years old, she had helped a little girl in need. She grew into a middle-class woman with a husband and two children. She had recently died and left something for her in her will. "Though," the lawyer said, "it's the most peculiar thing. She left you a pillow and a blanket."

– *Author Unknown*

A Glass of Milk

One day, a poor boy who was selling goods from door to door to pay his way through school, found he had only one thin dime left, and he was hungry.

He decided he would ask for a meal at the next house. However, he lost his nerve when a lovely young woman opened the door.

Instead of a meal he asked for a drink of water! She thought he looked hungry so brought him a large glass of milk. He drank it so slowly, and then asked, "How much do I owe you?"

"You don't owe me anything," she replied. "Mother has taught us never to accept pay for a kindness."

He said, "Then I thank you from my heart."

As Howard Kelly left that house, he not only felt stronger physically, but his faith in God and man was strong also. He had been ready to give up and quit.

Many year's later that same young woman became critically ill. The local doctors were baffled. They finally sent her to the big city, where they called in specialists to study her rare disease.

Dr. Howard Kelly was called in for the consultation. When he heard the name of the town she came from, a strange light filled his eyes.

Immediately he rose and went down the hall of the hospital to her room. Dressed in his doctor's gown he went in to see her. He recognized her at once.

He went back to the consultation room determined to do his best to save her life. From that day on he gave special attention to her case. After a long struggle, the battle was won.

Dr. Kelly requested the business office to pass the final bill to him for approval. He looked at it, then wrote something on the edge, and the bill was sent to her room.

She feared to open it, for she was sure it would take the rest of her life to pay for it all. Finally she looked, and something caught her attention on the side of the bill. She read these words, "Paid in full with one glass of milk"

(Signed) Dr. Howard Kelly.

Tears of joy flooded her eyes as her happy heart prayed: "Thank You, God, that Your love has spread broad through human hearts and hands."

There's a saying which goes something like this: "Bread cast on the water comes back to you." The good deed you do today may benefit you or someone you love at the least expected time. If you never see the deed again at least you will have made the world a better place - And, after all, isn't that what life is all about?

A Smell of Rain

A cold March wind danced around the dead of night in Dallas as the doctor walked into the small hospital room of Diana Blessing. Still groggy from surgery, her husband David held her hand as they braced themselves for the latest news.

That afternoon of March 10, 1991, complications had forced Diana, only24-weeks pregnant, to undergo an emergency cesarean to deliver the couple's new daughter, Danae Lu Blessing.

At 12 inches long and weighing only one pound and nine ounces, they already knew she was perilously premature. Still, the doctor's soft words dropped like bombs. "I don't think she's going to make it," he said, as kindly as he could. "There's only a 10-percent chance she will live through the night, and even then, if by some slim chance she does make it, her future could be a very cruel one."

Numb with disbelief, David and Diana listened as the doctor described the devastating problems Danae would likely face if she survived. She would never walk; she would never talk; she would probably be blind; she would certainly be prone to other catastrophic conditions from cerebral palsy to complete mental retardation; and on and on.

"No! No!" was all Diana could say. She and David with their 5-year-old son Dustin, had long dreamed of the day they would have a daughter to become a family of four. Now, within a matter of hours, that dream was slipping away.

Through the dark hours of morning as Danae held onto life by the thinnest thread. Diana slipped in and out of drugged sleep, growing more and more determined that their tiny daughter would live and live to be a healthy, happy young girl.

But David, fully awake and listening to additional dire details of their daughter's chances of ever leaving the hospital alive, much less healthy, knew he must confront his wife with the inevitable.

"David walked in and said that we needed to talk about making funeral arrangements," Diana remembers, "I felt so bad for him because he was doing everything, trying to include me in what was going on, but I just wouldn't listen, I couldn't listen."

I said, "No, that is not going to happen, no way! I don't care what the doctors say. Danae is not going to die! One day she will be just fine, and she will be coming home with us!"

As if willed to live by Diana's determination, Danae clung to life hour after hour, with the help of every medical machine and marvel her miniature body could endure but as those first days passed, a new agony set in for David and Diana. Because Danae's underdeveloped nervous system was essentially "raw", the lightest kiss or caress only intensified her discomfort - so they couldn't even cradle their tiny baby girl against their chests to offer the strength of their love.

All they could do, as Danae struggled alone beneath the ultra-violet light in the tangle of tubes and wires, was to pray that God would stay close to their precious little girl.

There was never a moment when Danae suddenly grew stronger. But as the weeks went by, she did slowly gain an ounce of weight here and an ounce of strength there.

At last, when Danae turned two months old, her parents were able to hold her in their arms for the very first time. And two months later though doctors continued to gently but grimly warn that her chances of surviving, much less living any kind of normal life, were next to zero.

Danae went home from the hospital, just as her mother had predicted.

Today, five years later, Danae is a petite but feisty young girl with glittering gray eyes and an unquenchable zest for life. She shows no signs, whatsoever, of any mental or physical impairments. Simply, she is everything a little girl can be and more but that happy ending is far from the end of her story.

One blistering afternoon in the summer of 1996 near her home in Irving, Texas, Danae was sitting in her mother's lap in the bleachers of a local ball park where her brother Dustin's baseball team was practicing. As always, Danae was chattering non-stop with her mother and several other adults sitting nearby when she suddenly fell silent.

Hugging her arms across her chest, Danae asked, "Do you smell that?" Smelling the air and detecting the approach of a thunderstorm, Diana replied, "Yes, it smells like rain."

Danae closed her eyes and again asked, "Do you smell that?" Once again, her mother replied, "Yes, I think we're about to get wet, it smells like rain."

Still caught in the moment, Danae shook her head, patted her thin shoulders with her small hands and loudly announced, "No, it smells like Him. It smells like God when you lay your head on His chest."

Tears blurred Diana's eyes as Danae then happily hopped down to play with the other children.

Before the rains came, her daughter's words confirmed what Diana and all the members of the extended Blessing family had known, at least in their hearts, all along.

During those long days and nights of her first two months of her life, when her nerves were too sensitive for them to touch her, God was holding Danae on His chest and it is His loving scent that she remembers so well.

– *Author Unknown*

Am I a Fireman Yet?

In Phoenix, Arizona, a 26-year-old mother stared down at her 6 year old son, who was dying of terminal leukemia.

Although her heart was filled with sadness, she also had a strong feeling of determination. Like any parent, she wanted her son to grow up and fulfill all his dreams. Now that was no longer possible.

The leukemia would see to that. But she still wanted her son's dream to come true. She took her son's hand and asked, "Billy, did you ever think about what you wanted to be once you grew up? Did you ever dream and wish what you would do with your life?"

"Mommy, I always wanted to be a fireman when I grew up." Mom smiled back and said, "Let's see if we can make your wish come true."

Later that day she went to her local fire Department in Phoenix, Arizona, where she met Fireman Bob, who had a heart as big as Phoenix. She explained her son's final wish and asked if it might be possible to give her 6 year-old son a ride around the block on a fire engine.

Fireman Bob said, "Look, we can do better than that. If you'll have your son ready at seven o'clock Wednesday morning, we'll make him an honorary Fireman for the whole day. He can come down to the fire station, eat with us, go out on all the fire calls, the whole nine yards!"

"And if you'll give us his sizes, we'll get a real fire uniform for him, with a real fire hat - not a toy one - with the emblem of the Phoenix Fire Department on it, a yellow slicker like we wear and rubber boots. They're all manufactured right here in Phoenix, so we can get them fast."

Three days later Fireman Bob picked up Billy, dressed him in his uniform and escorted him from his hospital bed to the waiting hook and ladder truck. Billy got to sit on the back of the truck and help steer it back to the fire station.

He was in heaven.

There were three fire calls in Phoenix that day and Billy got to go out on all three calls. He rode in the different fire engines, the Paramedics' van, and even the Fire Chief's car. He was also videotaped for the local news program.

Having his dream come true, with all the love and attention that was lavished upon him, so deeply touched Billy, that he lived three months longer than any doctor thought possible.

One night all of his vital signs began to drop dramatically and the head nurse, who believed in the hospice concept - that no one should die alone, began to call the family members to the hospital.

Then she remembered the day Billy had spent as a Fireman, so she called the Fire Chief and asked if it would be possible to send a fireman in uniform to the hospital to be with Billy as he made his transition.

The chief replied, "We can do better than that. We'll be there in five minutes. Will you please do me a favor?

"When you hear the sirens screaming and see the lights flashing, will you announce over the PA system that there is not a fire? It's the department coming to see one of its finest members one more time. And will you open the window to his room?"

About five minutes later a hook and ladder truck arrived at the hospital and extended its ladder up to Billy's third floor open window – 16 fire-fighters climbed up the ladder into Billy's room!

With his mother's permission, they hugged him and held him and told him how much they LOVED him.

With his dying breath, Billy looked up at the fire chief and said, "Chief, am I really a fireman now?"

"Billy, you are, and The Head Chief, Jesus, is holding your hand," the chief said.

With those words, Billy smiled and said, "I know, He's been holding my hand all day, and the angels have been singing."

He closed his eyes one last time.

An Old Man

In the faint light of the attic, an old man, tall and stooped, bent his great frame and made his way to a stack of boxes that sat near one of the little half-windows.

Brushing aside a wisp of cobwebs, he tilted the top box toward the light and began to carefully lift out one old photograph album after another. Eyes once bright but now dim searched longingly for the source that had drawn him here.

It began with the fond recollection of the love of his life, long gone, and somewhere in these albums was a photo of her he hoped to rediscover.

Silent as a mouse, he patiently opened the long-buried treasures and soon was lost in a sea of memories. Although his world had not stopped spinning when his wife left it, the past was more alive in his heart than his present aloneness.

Setting aside one of the dusty albums, he pulled from the box what appeared to be a journal from his grown son's childhood. He could not recall ever having seen it before, or that his son had ever kept a journal.

Opening the yellowed pages, he glanced over a short entry, and his lips curved in an unconscious smile. Even his eyes brightened as he read the words that spoke clear and sweet to his soul.

It was the voice of the little boy who had grown up far too fast in this very house, and whose voice had grown fainter and fainter over the years.

In the utter silence of the attic, the words of a guileless six-year-old worked their magic and carried the old man back to a time almost totally forgotten.

Entry after entry stirred a sentimental hunger in his heart like the longing a gardener feels in the winter for the fragrance of spring flowers. But it was accompanied by the painful memory that his son's simple recollections of those days were far different from his own. But how different?

Reminded that he had kept a daily journal of his business activities over the years, he closed his son's journal and turned to leave, having forgotten the cherished photo that originally triggered his search. He carried with him his son's journal.

In his den he opened a glass cabinet door, he reached in and pulled out an old business journal. Turning, he sat down at his desk and placed the two journals beside each other.

His was leather bound and engraved neatly with his name in gold, while his son's was tattered and the name "Jimmy" had been nearly scuffed from its surface. He ran a long skinny finger over the letters, as though he could restore what had been worn away with time and use.

As he opened his journal, the old man's eyes fell upon an inscription that stood out because it was so brief in comparison to other days. In his own neat handwriting were these words:

Wasted the whole day fishing with Jimmy. Didn't catch a thing.

With a deep sigh and a shaking hand, he took Jimmy's journal and found the boy's entry for the same day, June 4. Large scrawling letters pressed deeply in the paper read:

Went fishing with my dad. Best day of my life.

Someone once said, "I've never known anyone who, on their deathbed said. 'I wish I had spent more time at the office.'" Our Dash is a fleeting moment in time, and what we do with it is up to us.

Are You an Angel–or Something?

'Friends are God's way of taking care of us.'

This was written by a Metro Denver Hospice Physician:

I was driving home from a meeting this evening about 5, stuck in traffic on Colorado Blvd., and the car started to choke and splutter and die - I barely managed to coast, cursing, into a gas station, glad only that I would not be blocking traffic and would have a somewhat warm spot to wait for the tow truck. It wouldn't even turn over. Before I could make the call, I saw a woman walking out of the quickie mart building, and it looked like she slipped on some ice and fell into a gas pump, so I got out to see if she was okay.

When I got there, it looked more like she had been overcome by sobs than that she had fallen; she was a young woman who looked really haggard with dark circles under her eyes. She dropped something as I helped her up, and I picked it up to give it to her. It was a nickel.

At that moment, everything came into focus for me: the crying woman, the ancient Suburban crammed full of stuff with 3 kids in the back (1 in a car seat), and the gas pump reading $4.95.

I asked her if she was okay and if she needed help, and she just kept saying 'I don't want my kids to see me crying!,' so we stood on the other side of the pump from her car. She said she was driving to California and that things were very hard for her right now. So I asked, 'And you were praying?' That made her back away from me a little, but I assured her I was not a crazy person and said, 'He heard you, and He sent me.'

I took out my card and swiped it through the card reader on the pump so she could fill up her car completely, and while it was fueling, walked to the next door McDonald's and bought 2 big bags of food, some gift certificates for more, and a big cup of coffee. She gave the food to the kids in the car, who attacked it like wolves, and we stood by the pump eating fries and talking a little.

She told me her name, and that she lived in Kansas City. Her boyfriend left 2 months ago and she had not been able to make ends meet. She knew she wouldn't have money to pay rent Jan. 1, and finally, in desperation, had called her parents, with whom she had not spoken in about 5 years. They lived in California and said she could come live with them and try to get on her feet there.

So she packed up everything she owned in the car. She told the kids they were going to California for Christmas, but not that they were going to live there.

I gave her my gloves, a little hug and said a quick prayer with her for safety on the road. As I was walking over to my car, she said, 'So, are you like an angel or something?'

This definitely made me cry. I said, 'Sweetie, at this time of year angels are really busy, so sometimes God uses regular people.'

It was so incredible to be a part of someone else's miracle. And of course, you guessed it, when I got in my car it started right away and got me home with no problem. I'll put it in the shop tomorrow to check, but I suspect the mechanic won't find anything wrong.

Sometimes the angels fly close enough to you that you can hear the flutter of their wings.

Are You Jesus?

A few years ago a group of salesmen went to a regional sales convention in Chicago. They had assured their wives that they would be home in plenty of time for Friday night's dinner.

In their rush, with tickets and briefcases, one of these salesmen inadvertently kicked over a table which held a display of apples. Apples flew everywhere.

Without stopping or looking back, they all managed to reach the plane in time for their nearly-missed boarding–ALL BUT ONE!!! He paused, took a deep breath, got in touch with his feelings, and experienced a twinge of compassion for the girl whose apple stand had been overturned.

He told his buddies to go on without him, waved good-bye, told one of them to call his wife when they arrived at their home destination and explain his taking a later flight. Then he returned to the terminal where the apples were all over the terminal floor.

He was glad he did.

The 16-year-old girl was totally blind! She was softly crying, tears running down her cheeks in frustration, and at the same time helplessly groping for her spilled produce as the crowd swirled about her; no one stopping and no one to care for her plight.

The salesman knelt on the floor with her, gathered up the apples, put them back on the table and helped organize her display. As he did this, he noticed that many of them had become battered and bruised; these he set aside in another basket.

When he had finished, he pulled out his wallet and said to the girl, "Here, please take this $40 for the damage we did. Are you okay?" She nodded through her tears. He continued on with, "I hope we didn't spoil your day too badly."

As the salesman started to walk away, the bewildered blind girl called out to him, "Mister, . . ." He paused and turned to look back into those blind eyes. She continued, "Are you Jesus?"

He stopped in mid-stride, and he wondered. Then slowly he made his way to catch the later flight with that question burning and bouncing about in his soul: "Are you Jesus?"

Do people mistake you for Jesus? That's our destiny, is it not? To be so much like Jesus that people cannot tell the difference as we live and interact with a world that is blind to His love, life and grace.

Burned Biscuits

When I was a kid, my Mom liked to make breakfast food for dinner every now and then. And I remember one night in particular when she had made breakfast after a long, hard day at work.

On that evening so long ago, my Mom placed a plate of eggs, sausage and extremely burned biscuits in front of my dad. I remember waiting to see if anyone noticed!

Yet all my dad did was reach for his biscuit, smile at my Mom and ask me how my day was at school. I don't remember what I told him that night, but I do remember watching him smear butter and jelly on that ugly burned biscuit. He ate every bite of that thing. . . never made a face nor uttered a word about it!

When I got up from the table that evening, I remember hearing my Mom apologize to my dad for burning the biscuits. And I'll never forget what he said: "Honey, I love burned biscuits every now and then."

Later that night, I went to kiss Daddy good night and I asked him if he really liked his biscuits burned. He wrapped me in his arms and said, "Your Momma put in a hard day at work today and she's real tired. And besides - a little burned biscuit never hurt anyone!"

As I've grown older, I've thought about that many times. Life is full of imperfect things and imperfect people. I'm not the best at hardly anything, and I forget birthdays and anniversaries just like everyone else. But what I've learned over the years is that learning to accept each other's faults - and choosing to celebrate each others differences - is one of the most important keys to creating a healthy, growing, and lasting relationship.

And that's my prayer for you today. . . that you will learn to take the good, the bad, and the ugly parts of your life and lay them at the feet of God. Because in the end, He's the only One who will be able to give you a relationship where a burnt biscuit isn't a deal-breaker!

"Don't put the key to your happiness in someone else's pocket - keep it in your own."

So, please pass me a biscuit, and yes, the burned one will do just fine.

Captain Kangaroo – Remember Him?

Captain Kangaroo passed away on January 23, 2004 at age 76, which is odd, because he always looked to be 76. (DOB: 6/27/27)His death reminded me of the following story.

Some people have been a bit offended that the actor, Lee Marvin, is buried in a grave alongside 3 and 4-star generals at Arlington National Cemetery His marker gives his name, rank (PVT) and service (USMC). Nothing else. Here's a guy who was only a famous movie star who served his time, why the heck does he rate burial with these guys? Well, following is the amazing answer:

I always liked Lee Marvin, but didn't know the extent of his Corps experiences.

In a time when many Hollywood stars served their country in the armed forces often in rear echelon posts where they were carefully protected, only to be trotted out to perform for the cameras in war bond promotions, Lee Marvin was a genuine hero. He won the Navy Cross at Iwo Jima There is only one higher Naval award. . . the Medal Of Honor!

If that is a surprising comment on the true character of the man, he credits his sergeant with an even greater show of bravery.

Dialog from "The Tonight Show with Johnny Carson": His guest was Lee Marvin. . . Johnny said, "Lee, I'll bet a lot of people are unaware that you were a Marine in the initial landing at Iwo Jima and that during the course of that action you earned the Navy Cross and were severely wounded."

"Yeah, yeah. . . I got shot square in the bottom and they gave me the Cross for securing a hot spot about halfway up Suribachi. Bad thing about getting shot up on a mountain is guys getting shot hauling you down. But, Johnny, at Iwo I served under the bravest man I ever knew. We both got the Cross the same day, but what he did for his Cross made mine look cheap in comparison. That dumb guy actually stood up on Red beach and directed his troops to move forward and get off the beach. Bullets flying by, with mortar rounds landing everywhere and he stood there as the main target of gunfire so that he could get his men to safety. He did this on more than one occasion because his men's safety was more important than his own life.

That Sergeant and I have been lifelong friends. When they brought me off Suribachi we passed the Sergeant and he lit a smoke and passed it to me, lying on my belly on the litter and said, "Where'd they get you Lee?" "Well Bob, if you make it home before me, tell Mom to sell the outhouse!"

Johnny, I'm not lying, Sergeant Keeshan was the bravest man I ever knew.

The Sergeant's name is Bob Keeshan. You and the world know him as "Captain Kangaroo."

On another note, there was this wimpy little man (who has passed away) on PBS, gentle and quiet. Mr. Rogers is another of those you would least suspect of being anything but what he now portrays to our youth. But Mr. Rogers was a U.S. Navy Seal, combat-proven in Vietnam with over twenty-five confirmed kills to his name. He wore a long-sleeved sweater on TV, to cover the many tattoos on his forearm and biceps. He was a master in small arms and hand-to-hand combat, able to disarm or kill in a heartbeat

After the war Mr. Rogers became an ordained Presbyterian minister and therefore a pacifist. Vowing to never harm another human and also dedicating the rest of his life to trying to help lead children on the right path in life. He hid away the tattoos and his past life and won our hearts with his quiet wit and charm.

America's real heroes don't flaunt what they did; they quietly go about their day-to-day lives, doing what they do best. They earned our respect and the freedoms that we all enjoy.

Look around and see if you can find one of those heroes in your midst.

Often, they are the ones you'd least suspect, but would most like to have on your side if anything ever happened.

Take the time to thank anyone that has fought for our freedom. With encouragement they could be the next Captain Kangaroo or Mr. Rogers.

Carl's Garden

Carl was a quiet man. He didn't talk much. He would always greet you with a big smile and a firm handshake. Even after living in our neighborhood for over 50 years, no one could really say they knew him very well.

Before his retirement, he took the bus to work each morning. The lone sight of him walking down the street often worried us. He had a slight limp from a bullet wound received in WW II. Watching him, we worried that although he had survived WW II, he may not make it through our changing uptown neighborhood with its ever-increasing random violence, gangs, and drug activity.

When he saw the flyer at our local church asking for volunteers for caring for the gardens behind the minister's residence, he responded in his characteristically unassuming manner. Without fanfare, he just signed up.

He was well into his 87th year when the very thing we had always feared finally happened.

He was almost finished with his watering for the day when three gang members approached him. Ignoring their attempt to intimidate him, he simply asked,

"Would you like a drink from the hose?"

The tallest and toughest-looking of the three said, "Yeah, sure", with a malevolent little smile. As Carl offered the hose to him, the other two grabbed Carl's arm, throwing him down. As the hose snaked crazily over the ground, dousing everything in its way, Carl's assailants stole his retirement watch and his wallet, and then fled.

Carl tried to get himself up, but he had been thrown down on his bad leg. He lay there trying to gather himself as the minister came running to help him. Although the minister had witnessed the attack from his window, he couldn't get there fast enough to stop it.

"Carl, are you okay? Are you hurt?" the minister kept asking as he helped Carl to his feet. Carl just passed a hand over his brow and sighed, shaking his head.

"Just some punk kids. I hope they'll wise-up someday." His wet clothes clung to his slight frame as he bent to pick up the hose. He adjusted the nozzle again and started to water again.

Confused and a little concerned, the minister asked, "Carl, what are you doing?"

"I've got to finish my watering. It's been very dry lately", came the calm reply. Satisfying himself that Carl really was all right, the minister could only marvel. Carl was a man from a different time and place.

A few weeks later the three returned. Just as before their threat was unchallenged. Carl again offered them a drink form his hose. This time they didn't rob him. They wrenched the hose from his hand and drenched him head to foot in the icy water.

When they had finished their humiliation of him, they sauntered off down the street, throwing catcalls and curses, falling over one another laughing at the hilarity of what they had just done.

Carl just watched them. Then he turned toward the warmth giving sun, picked up his hose, and went on with his watering.

The summer was quickly fading into fall. Carl was doing some tilling when he was startled by the sudden approach of someone behind him. He stumbled and fell into some evergreen branches. As he struggled to regain his footing, he turned to see the tall leader of his summer tormenters reaching down for him. He braced himself for the expected attack. "Don't worry old man, I'm not gonna hurt you this time." The young man spoke softly, still offering the tattooed and scarred hand to Carl.

As he helped Carl get up, the man pulled a crumpled bag from his pocket and handed it to Carl. "What's this?" Carl asked.

"It's your stuff," the man explained. "It's your stuff back. Even the money in your wallet."

"I don't understand," Carl said. "Why would you help me now?"

The man shifted his feet, seeming embarrassed and ill at ease. "I learned something from you", he said. "I ran with that gang and hurt people like you. We picked you because you were old and we knew we could do it. But every time we came and did something to you, instead of yelling and fighting back, you tried to give us a drink. You didn't hate us for hating you. You kept showing love against our hate." He stopped for a moment. "I couldn't sleep after we stole your stuff, so here it is back."

He paused for another awkward moment, not knowing what more there was to say. "That bag's my way of saying thanks for straightening me out, I guess." And with that, he walked off down the street.

Carl looked down at the sack in his hands and gingerly opened it. He took out his retirement watch and put it back on his wrist. Opening his wallet, he checked for his wedding photo. He gazed for a moment at the young bride that still smiled back at him from all those years ago.

He died one cold day after Christmas that winter. Many people attended his funeral in spite of the weather. In particular the minister noticed a tall young man that he didn't know sitting quietly in a distant corner of the church.

The minister spoke of Carl's garden as a lesson in life. In a voice made thick with unshed tears, he said, "Do your best and make your garden as beautiful as you can. We will never forget Carl and his garden."

The following spring another flyer went up. It read: "Person needed to care for Carl's garden." The flyer went unnoticed by the busy parishioners until one day when a knock was heard at the minister's office door. Opening the door, the minister saw a pair of scarred and tattooed hands holding the flyer. "I believe this is my job, if you'll have me," the young man said.

The minister recognized him as the same young man who had returned the stolen watch and wallet to Carl. He knew that Carl's kindness had turned this man's life around. As the minister handed him the keys to the garden shed, he said, "Yes, go take care of Carl's garden and honor him."

The man went to work and, over the next several years, he tended the flowers and vegetables just as Carl had done. In that time, he went to college, got married and became a prominent member of the community. But he never forgot his promise to Carl's memory and kept the garden as beautiful as he thought Carl would have kept it.

One day he approached the new minister and told him that he couldn't care for the garden any longer. He explained with a shy and happy smile, "My wife just had a baby boy last night, and she's bringing him home on Saturday."

"Well, congratulations!" said the minister, as he was handed the garden shed keys. "That's wonderful! What's the baby's name?"

It was Carl.

– *Author Unknown*

Communion on the Moon: July 20, 1969

(This is an article by Eric Metaxas)

On July the 20, 1969 two human beings changed history by walking on the surface of the moon. But what happened before Buzz Aldrin and Neil Armstrong exited the Lunar Module is perhaps even more amazing, if only because so few people know about it. I'm talking about the fact that Buzz Aldrin took communion on the surface of the moon.

Some months after his return, he wrote about it in Guideposts magazine.

And a few years ago I had the privilege of meeting him myself. I asked him about it and he confirmed the story to me, and I wrote about in my book *Everything You Always Wanted to Know About God (But Were Afraid to Ask)*.

The background to the story is that Aldrin was an elder at his Presbyterian Church in Texas during this period in his life, and knowing that he would soon be doing something unprecedented in human history, he felt he should mark the occasion somehow, and he asked his minister to help him.

And so the minister consecrated a communion wafer and a small vial of communion wine. And Buzz Aldrin took them with him out of the Earth's orbit and on to the surface of the moon.

He and Armstrong had only been on the lunar surface for a few minutes when Aldrin made the following public statement: "This is the LM pilot. I'd like to take this opportunity to ask every person listening in, whoever and wherever they may be, to pause for a moment and contemplate the events of the past few hours and to give thanks in his or her own way."

He then ended radio communication and there, on the silent surface of the moon, 250,000 miles from home, he read a verse from the Gospel of John, and he took communion.

Here is his own account of what happened:

"In the radio blackout, I opened the little plastic packages which contained the bread and the wine. I poured the wine into the chalice our church had given me.

In the one-sixth gravity of the moon, the wine slowly curled and gracefully came up the side of the cup. Then I read the scripture, 'I am the vine, you are the branches. Whosoever abides in me will bring forth much fruit. Apart from me you can do nothing.'"

I had intended to read my communion passage back to earth, but at the last minute [they] had requested that I not do this. NASA was already embroiled in a legal battle with Madelyn Murray O'Hare, the celebrated opponent of religion, over the Apollo 8 crew reading from Genesis while orbiting the moon at Christmas. I agreed reluctantly.

I ate the tiny Host and swallowed the wine. I gave thanks for the intelligence and spirit that had brought two young pilots to the Sea of Tranquility. It was interesting for me to think: the very first liquid ever poured on the moon, and the very first food eaten there, were the communion elements.

And of course, it's interesting to think that some of the first words spoken on the moon were the words of Jesus Christ, who made the Earth and the heavens; the sun and THE MOON.

Curtain Rods

She spent the first day packing her belongings into boxes, crates and suitcases.

On the second day, she had the movers come and collect her things.

On the third day, she sat down for the last time at their beautiful dining room table by candle-light, put on some soft background music, and feasted on a pound of shrimp, a jar of caviar, and a bottle of spring-water.

When she had finished, she went into each and every room and deposited a few half-eaten shrimp shells dipped in caviar into the hollow of the curtain rods. She then cleaned up the kitchen and left.

When the husband returned with his new girlfriend, all was bliss for the first few days.

Then slowly, the house began to smell. They tried everything; cleaning, mopping and airing the place out. Vents were checked for dead rodents and carpets were steam cleaned.

Air fresheners were hung everywhere. Exterminators were brought in to set off gas canisters, during which they had to move out for a few days and in the end they even paid to replace the expensive wool carpeting. Nothing worked.

People stopped coming over to visit. Repairmen refused to work in the house. The maid quit. Finally, they could not take the stench any longer and decided to move.

A month later, even though they had cut their price in half, they could not find a buyer for their stinky house.

Word got out and eventually even the local realtors refused to return their calls.

Finally, they had to borrow a huge sum of money from the bank to purchase a new place.

The ex-wife called the man and asked how things were going. He told her the saga of the rotting house. She listened politely and said that she missed her old home terribly and would be willing to reduce her divorce settlement in exchange for getting the house back.

Knowing his ex-wife had no idea how bad the smell was, he agreed on a price that was about 1/10th of what the house had been worth, but only if she were to sign the papers that very day. She agreed and within the hour his lawyers delivered the paperwork.

A week later the man and his girlfriend stood smiling as they watched the moving company pack everything to take to their new home.

And to spite the ex-wife, they even took the curtain rods!!!!!!

Do You Believe in Easter?

Edith Burns was a wonderful Christian who lived in San Antonio, Texas. She was the patient of a doctor by the name of Will Phillips. Dr. Phillips was a gentle doctor who saw patients as people. His favorite patient was Edith Burns.

One morning he went to his office with a heavy heart and it was because of Edith Burns.

When he walked into that waiting room, there sat Edith with her big black Bible in her lap earnestly talking to a young mother sitting beside her.

Edith Burns had a habit of introducing herself in this way: "Hello, my name is Edith Burns. Do you believe in Easter?" Then she would explain the meaning of Easter, and many times people would be saved.

Dr. Phillips walked into that office and there he saw the head nurse, Beverly. Beverly had first met Edith when she was taking her blood pressure

Edith began by saying, "My name is Edith Burns. Do you believe in Easter?"

Beverly said, "Why yes I do."

Edith said, "Well, what do you believe about Easter?"

Beverly said, "Well, it's all about egg hunts, going to church, and dressing up."

Edith kept pressing her about the real meaning of Easter, and finally led her to a saving knowledge of Jesus Christ.

Dr. Phillips said, "Beverly, don't call Edith into the office quite yet. I believe there is another delivery taking place in the waiting room."

After being called back in the doctor's office, Edith sat down and when she took a look at the doctor she said, "Dr. Will, why are you so sad? Are you reading your Bible? Are you praying?"

Dr. Phillips said gently, "Edith, I'm the doctor and you're the patient." With a heavy heart he said, "Your lab report came back and it says you have cancer, and Edith, you're not going to live very long."

Edith said, "Why Will Phillips, shame on you. Why are you so sad? Do you think God makes mistakes? You have just told me I'm going to see my precious Lord Jesus, my husband, and my friends. You have just told me that I am going to celebrate Easter forever, and here you are having difficulty giving me my ticket!"

Dr. Phillips thought to himself, "What a magnificent woman this Edith Burns is!"

Edith continued coming to Dr. Phillips. Christmas came and the office was closed through January 3rd. On the day the office opened, Edith did not show up.

Later that afternoon, Edith called Dr. Phillips and said she would have to be moving her story to the hospital and said, "Will, I'm very near home, so would you make sure that they put women in here next to me in my room who need to know about Easter."

Well, they did just that and women began to come in and share that room with Edith. Many women were saved. Everybody on that floor from staff to patients were so excited about Edith, that they started calling her Edith Easter; that is everyone except Phyllis Cross, the head nurse.

Phyllis made it plain that she wanted nothing to do with Edith because she was a "religious nut". She had been a nurse in an army hospital. She had seen it all and heard it all. She was the original G.I. Jane. She had been married three times, she was hard, cold, and did everything by the book.

One morning the two nurses who were to attend to Edith were sick.

Edith had the flu and Phyllis Cross had to go in and give her a shot. When she walked in, Edith had a big smile on her face and said, "Phyllis, God loves you and I love you, and I have been praying for you."

Phyllis Cross said, "Well, you can quit praying for me, it won't work. I'm not interested."

Edith said, "Well, I will pray and I have asked God not to let me go home until you come into the family."

Phyllis Cross said, "Then you will never die because that will never happen", and curtly walked out of the room.

Every day Phyllis Cross would walk into the room and Edith would say, "God loves you Phyllis and I love you, and I'm praying for you."

One day Phyllis Cross said she was literally drawn to Edith's room like a magnet would draw iron. She sat down on the bed and Edith said, "I'm so glad you have come, because God told me that today is your special day"

Phyllis Cross said, "Edith, you have asked everybody here the question, "Do you believe in Easter but you have never asked me."

Edith said, "Phyllis, I wanted to many times, but God told me to wait until you asked, and now that you have asked." Edith Burns took her Bible and shared with Phyllis Cross the Easter Story of the death, burial and resurrection of Jesus Christ. Edith said, "Phyllis, do you believe in Easter? Do you believe that Jesus Christ is alive and that He wants to live in your heart?"

Phyllis Cross said, "Oh I want to believe that with all of my heart, and I do want Jesus in my life "Right there, Phyllis Cross prayed and invited Jesus Christ into her heart. For the first time Phyllis Cross did not walk out of a hospital room, she was carried out on the wings of angels.

Two days later, Phyllis Cross came in and Edith said,

"Do you know what day it is?"

Phyllis Cross said, "Why Edith, it's Good Friday."

Edith said, "Oh, no, for you every day is Easter. Happy Easter Phyllis!"

Two days later, on Easter Sunday, Phyllis Cross came into work, did some of her duties and then went down to the flower shop and got some Easter lilies because she wanted to go up to see Edith and give her some Easter lilies and wish her a Happy Easter.

When she walked into Edith's room, Edith was in bed. That big black Bible was on her lap. Her hands were in that Bible. There was a sweet smile on her face. When Phyllis Cross went to pick up Edith's hand, she realized Edith was dead. Her left hand was on John 14: "In my Father's house are many mansions. I go to prepare a place for you, I will come again and receive you to Myself, that where I am, there you may be also."

Her right finger was soundly resting on Revelation 21:4, "And God will wipe away every tear from their eyes, there shall be no more death nor sorrow, nor crying; and there shall be no more pain, for the former things have passed away."

Phyllis Cross took one look at that dead body, and then lifted her face toward heaven, and with tears streaming down her cheeks, said, "Happy Easter, Edith - Happy Easter!"

Phyllis Cross left Edith's body, walked out of the room, and over to a table where two student nurses were sitting.

She said, "My name is Phyllis Cross. Do you believe in Easter?"

Forrest Gump

Forrest Gump dies and goes to Heaven. He is met at the Pearly Gate by St. Peter himself.

The gates are closed, however, and Forrest approaches the gatekeeper. St. Peter says "Well, Forrest, it's certainly good to see you. We have heard so many good things about you. I must inform you that the place is filling up fast, and we've been giving an entrance quiz for everyone. The tests are short, but you need to pass before you can get into Heaven."

Forrest responds "It sure is good to be here, St. Peter. I was looking forward to this. Nobody ever told me about any entrance exam. Sure hope the test ain't too hard; Life was a big enough test as it was."

St. Peter goes on, "I know, Forrest, but the test is only three questions:

1. What days of the week begin with the letter T?

2. How many seconds are there in a year?

3. What is God's first name?"

Forrest goes away to think the questions over. He returns the next day and goes up to St. Peter to try to answer the exam questions.

St. Peter waves him up and says, "Now that you have had a chance to think the questions over, tell me your answers".

Forrest says, "Well, the first one how many days of the week begin with the letter 'T?' Shucks, that one's easy. That'd be Today and Tomorrow."

The Saint's eyes open wide and he exclaims "Forrest! That's not what I was thinking, but . . . you do have a point though, and I guess I didn't specify, so I will give you credit for that answer."

"How about the next one?" "How many seconds in a year?"

"Now that one's harder", says Forrest, "but I thought and thought about that and I guess the only answer can be twelve."

Astounded, St. Peter says "Twelve! Twelve! Forrest, how in Heaven's name could you come up with twelve seconds in a year?

Forest says "Aw, come on, St Peter, there's gotta be twelve, January second, February second, March second. . "

"Hold it" interrupts St. Peter. "I see where you're going with it. I guess I see your point, though that wasn't quite what I had in mind, but I'll give you credit for that one too. Let's go on with the next and final question, "Can you tell me God's first name?"

Forrest replied, "Andy."

When St. Peter asked how in the world he came up with the name Andy. Forrest replied, "You know, St. Peter, that song we sing in church: "Andy walks with me, Andy talks with me. Andy tells me I am His own."

The lesson: THERE IS ALWAYS ANOTHER POINT OF VIEW, and just because another person doesn't see things the same way or understand the same way that you do, does not mean that it's wrong.

– *Author Unknown*

God Bless This Airline Captain

My lead flight attendant came to me and said, "We have an H.R. on this flight." (H.R. stands for human remains.) "Are they military?" I asked.

"Yes," she said.

"Is there an escort?" I asked.

"Yes, I already assigned him a seat."

"Would you please tell him to come to the flight deck. You can board him early," I said.

A short while later, a young army sergeant entered the flight deck. He was the image of the perfectly dressed soldier. He introduced himself and I asked him about his soldier. The escorts of these fallen soldiers talk about them as if they are still alive and still with us.

"My soldier is on his way back to Virginia," he said. He proceeded to answer my questions, but offered no words.

I asked him if there was anything I could do for him and he said no. I told him that he had the toughest job in the military and that I appreciated the work that he does for the families of our fallen soldiers. The first officer and I got up out of our seats to shake his hand. He left the flight deck to find his seat.

We completed our pre-flight checks, pushed back and performed an uneventful departure. About 30 minutes into our flight I received a call from the lead flight attendant in the cabin. "I just found out the family of the soldier we are carrying, is on board," she said.

She then proceeded to tell me that the father, mother, wife and 2-year-old daughter were escorting their son, husband, and father home. The family was upset because they were unable to see the container that the soldier was in before we left.

We were on our way to a major hub at which the family was going to wait four hours for the connecting flight home to Virginia.

The father of the soldier told the flight attendant that knowing his son was below him in the cargo compartment and being unable to see him was too much for him and the family to bear. He had asked the flight attendant if there was anything that could be done to allow them to see him upon our arrival. The family wanted to be outside by the cargo door to watch the soldier being taken off the airplane.

I could hear the desperation in the flight attendant's voice when she asked me if there was anything I could do. "I'm on it," I said. I told her that I would get back to her.

Airborne communication with my company normally occurs in the form of e-mail like messages. I decided to bypass this system and contact my flight dispatcher directly on a secondary radio. There is a radio operator in the operations control center who connects you to the telephone of the dispatcher. I was in direct contact with the dispatcher. I explained the situation I had on board with the family and what it was the family wanted. He said he understood and that he would get back to me.

Two hours went by and I had not heard from the dispatcher. We were going to get busy soon and I needed to know what to tell the family. I sent a text message asking for an update. I saved the return message from the dispatcher and the following is the text:

"Captain, sorry it has taken so long to get back to you. There is policy on this now and I had to check on a few things. Upon your arrival a dedicated escort team will meet the aircraft. The team will escort the family to the ramp and plane side. A van will be used to load the remains with a secondary van for the family. The family will be taken to their departure area and escorted into the terminal where the remains can be seen on the ramp. It is a private area for the family only. When the connecting aircraft arrives, the family will be escorted onto the ramp and plane side to watch the remains being loaded for the final leg home. Captain, most of us here in flight control are veterans. Please pass our condolences on to the family. Thanks."

I sent a message back telling flight control thanks for a good job. I printed out the message and gave it to the lead flight attendant to pass on to the father. The lead flight attendant was very thankful and told me, "You have no idea how much this will mean to them."

Things started getting busy for the descent, approach and landing. After landing, we cleared the runway and taxied to the ramp area. The ramp is huge with 15 gates on either side of the alleyway. It is always a busy area with aircraft maneuvering every which way to enter and exit. When we entered the ramp and checked in with the ramp controller, we were told that all traffic was being held for us.

"There is a team in place to meet the aircraft," we were told.

It looked like it was all coming together, then I realized that once we turned the seat belt sign off, everyone would stand up at once and delay the family from getting off the airplane. As we approached our gate, I asked the copilot to tell the ramp controller we were going to stop short of the gate to make an announcement to the passengers. He did that and the ramp controller said, "Take your time."

I stopped the aircraft and set the parking brake. I pushed the public address button and said, "Ladies and gentlemen, this is your Captain speaking. I have stopped short of our gate to make a special announcement. We have a passenger on board who deserves our honor and respect. His Name is Private XXXXXX, a soldier who recently lost his life. Private XXXXXX is under your feet in the cargo hold. Escorting him today is Army Sergeant XXXXXXX. Also on board are his father, mother, wife, and daughter. Your entire flight crew is asking for all passengers to remain in their seats to allow the family to exit the aircraft first. Thank you."

We continued the turn to the gate, came to a stop and started our shutdown procedures. A couple of minutes later I opened the cockpit door. I found the two forward flight attendants crying, something you just do not see. I was told that after we came to a stop, every passenger on the aircraft stayed in their seats, waiting for the family to exit the aircraft.

When the family got up and gathered their things, a passenger slowly started to clap his hands. Moments later more passengers joined in and soon the entire aircraft was clapping. Words of "God Bless You, I'm sorry, Thank you, Be proud," and other kind words were uttered to the family as they made their way down the aisle and out of the airplane. They were escorted down to the ramp to finally be with their loved one.

Many of the passengers disembarking thanked me for the announcement I had made. "They were just words," I told them. "I could say them over and over again, but nothing I say will bring back that brave soldier."

I respectfully ask that all of you reflect on this event and the sacrifices that millions of our men and women have made to ensure our freedom and safety in these United States of AMERICA.

Footnote:

As a Viet Nam Veteran I can only think of all the veterans, including the ones that rode below the deck on their way home and how they were treated. When I read things like this I am proud that our country has not turned their backs on our soldiers returning from the various war zones today and give them the respect they so deserve.

I know everyone who has served their country who reads this will have tears in their eyes, including me.

Grandma's Hands

Grandma, some ninety plus years, sat feebly on the patio bench. She didn't move, just sat with her head down staring at her hands.

When I sat down beside her she didn't acknowledge my presence and the longer I sat I wondered if she was OK. Finally, not really wanting to disturb her but wanting to check on her at the same time, I asked her if she was OK. She raised her head and looked at me and smiled. "Yes, I'm fine, thank you for asking," she said in a clear voice strong.

"I didn't mean to disturb you, grandma, but you were just sitting here staring at your hands and I wanted to make sure you were OK," I explained to her.

"Have you ever looked at your hands," she asked. "I mean really looked at your hands?"

I slowly opened my hands and stared down at them. I turned them over, palms up and then palms down. No, I guess I had never really looked at my hands as I tried to figure out the point she was making.

Grandma smiled and related this story:

"Stop and think for a moment about the hands you have, how they have served you well throughout your years. These hands, though wrinkled shriveled and weak have been the tools I have used all my life to reach out and grab and embrace life.

"They braced and caught my fall when as a toddler I crashed upon the floor. They put food in my mouth and clothes on my back. As a child, my mother taught me to fold them in prayer. They tied my shoes and pulled on my boots.

"They have been dirty, scraped and raw, swollen and bent. They were uneasy and clumsy when I tried to hold my newborn son. and they loved a Man someone special. They wrote my letters to him and trembled and shook when I buried my parents and spouse.

"They have held my children and grandchildren, consoled neighbors, and shook in fists of anger when I didn't understand. They have covered my face, combed my hair, and washed and cleansed the rest of my body. They have been sticky and wet, bent and broken, dried and raw. And to this day when not much of anything else of me works real well these hands hold me up, lay me down, and again continue to fold in prayer.

"These hands are the mark of where I've been and the ruggedness of life. But more importantly it will be these hands that God will reach out and take when he leads me home. And with my hands He will lift me to His side and there I will use these hands to touch the face of Christ."

I will never look at my hands the same again. But I remember God reached out and took my grandma's hands and led her home.

When my hands are hurt or sore or when I stroke the face of my children and husband I think of grandma. I know she has been stroked and caressed and held by the hands of God.

I, too, want to touch the face of God and feel His hands upon my face.

– Author Unknown

How Do You Spell Fix?

When I was a young boy, my father had one of the first telephones in our neighborhood. I remember the polished, old case fastened to the wall. The shiny receiver hung on the side of the box. I was too little to reach the telephone, but used to listen with fascination when my mother talked to it.

Then I discovered that somewhere inside the wonderful device lived an amazing person. Her name was "Information Please" and there was nothing she did not know. Information Please could supply anyone's number and the correct time.

My personal experience with the genie-in-a-bottle came one day while my mother was visiting a neighbor. Amusing myself at the tool bench in the basement, I whacked my finger with a hammer, the pain was terrible, but there seemed no point in crying because there was no one home to give sympathy.

I walked around the house sucking my throbbing finger, finally arriving at the stairway. The telephone! Quickly, I ran for the footstool in the parlor and dragged it to the landing. Climbing up, I unhooked the receiver in the parlor and held it to my ear.

"Information, please" I said into the mouthpiece just above my head.

A click or two and a small clear voice spoke into my ear.

"Information."

"I hurt my finger." I wailed into the phone, the tears came readily enough now that I had an audience.

"Isn't your mother home?" came the question.

"Nobody's home but me," I blubbered.

"Are you bleeding?" the voice asked.

"No,"

I replied. "I hit my finger with the hammer and it hurts."

"Can you open the icebox?" she asked.

I said I could.

"Then chip off a little bit of ice and hold it to your finger," said the voice.

After that, I called "Information Please" for everything. I asked her for help with my geography, and she told me where Philadelphia was. She helped me with my math. She told me my pet chipmunk that I had caught in the park just the day before, would eat fruit and nuts.

Then, there was the time Petey, our pet canary, died. I called, "Information Please," and told her the sad story. She listened, and then said things grown-ups say to soothe a child. But I was not consoled. I asked her, "Why is it that birds should sing so beautifully and bring joy to all families, only to end up as a heap of feathers on the bottom of a cage?"

She must have sensed my deep concern, for she said quietly, "Wayne, always remember that there are other worlds to sing in."

Somehow I felt better.

Another day I was on the telephone, "Information Please."

"Information," said in the now familiar voice. "How do I spell fix?", I asked.

All this took place in a small town in the Pacific Northwest. When I was nine years old, we moved across the country to Boston. I missed my friend very much.

"Information Please" belonged in that old wooden box back home and I somehow never thought of trying the shiny new phone that sat on the table in the hall. As I grew into my teens, the memories of those childhood conversations never really left me.

Often, in moments of doubt and perplexity I would recall the serene sense of security I had then. I appreciated now how patient, understanding, and kind she was to have spent her time on a little boy.

A few years later, on my way west to college, my plane put down in Seattle. I had about a half-hour or so between planes. I spent 15 minutes or so on the phone with my sister, who lived there now. Then without thinking what I was doing, I dialed my hometown operator and said, "Information Please."

Miraculously, I heard the small, clear voice I knew so well.

"Information."

I hadn't planned this, but I heard myself saying,

"Could you please tell me how to spell fix?"

There was a long pause. Then came the soft spoken answer, "I guess your finger must have healed by now."

I laughed, "So it's really you," I said. "I wonder if you have any idea how much you meant to me during that time?"

I wonder," she said, "if you know how much your call meant to me. I never had any children and I used to look forward to your calls."

I told her how often I had thought of her over the years and I asked if I could call her again when I came back to visit my sister.

"Please do", she said. "Just ask for Sally."

Three months later I was back in Seattle . A different voice answered, "Information."

I asked for Sally.

"Are you a friend?" she said.

"Yes, a very old friend," I answered.

"I'm sorry to have to tell you this," she said. "Sally had been working part time the last few years because she was sick. She died five weeks ago."

Before I could hang up, she said, "Wait a minute, did you say your name was Wayne ?"

"Yes." I answered.

"Well, Sally left a message for you.

She wrote it down in case you called.

Let me read it to you."

The note said,

"Tell him there are other worlds to sing in.

He'll know what I mean."

I thanked her and hung up. I knew what Sally meant.

Never underestimate the impression you may make on others.

Whose life have you touched today?

I Was That Father

An elderly man stepped up to the pulpit and began to speak.

"A father, his son, and a friend of his son were sailing off the pacific coast," he began, "when a fast approaching storm blocked any attempt to get back to the shore.

"The waves were so high, that even though the father was an experienced sailor, he could not keep the boat upright and the three were swept into the ocean as the boat capsized."

The old man hesitated for a moment, making eye contact with two teenagers who were, for the first time since the service began, looking somewhat interested in his story.

The aged minister continued with his story, "grabbing a rescue line, the father had to make the most excruciating decision of his life: to which boy would he throw the other end of the life line.

"He only had seconds to make the decision. The father knew that his son was a Christian and he, also, knew that his son's friend was not. The agony of his decision could not be matched by the torrent of waves.

"As the father yelled out, 'I love you, son!' he threw out the life line to his son's friend. By the time the father had pulled the friend back to the capsized boat, his son had disappeared beneath the raging swells into the black of night. His body was never recovered."

By this time, the two teenagers were sitting up straight in the pew, anxiously waiting for the next words to come out of the old minister's mouth.

"The father," he continued, "knew his son would step into eternity with Jesus and he could not bear the thought of his son's friend stepping into an eternity without Jesus. Therefore, He sacrificed his son to save the son's friend."

How great is the love of God that He should do the same for us. Our heavenly Father sacrificed His only begotten Son that we could be saved. I urge you to accept His offer to rescue you and take a hold of the life line He is throwing out to you in this service."

With that, the old man turned and sat back down in his chair as silence filled the room.

The pastor again walked slowly to the pulpit and delivered a brief sermon with an invitation at the end. However, no one responded to the appeal.

Within minutes after the service ended, the two teenagers were at the old man's side. "That was a nice story," politely stated one of them, "but I don't think it was very realistic for a father to give up his only son's life in hopes that the other boy would become a Christian."

"Well, you've got a point there," the old man replied, glancing down at his worn bible. A big smile broadened his narrow face. He once again looked up at the boys and said, "It sure isn't very realistic, is it? But, I'm standing here today to tell you that story gives me a glimpse of what it must have been like for God to give up His Son for me.

You see . . . I was that father and your pastor is my son's friend."

Is Your Hut Burning?

The only survivor of a shipwreck was washed up on a small, uninhabited island. He prayed feverishly for God to rescue him, and every day he scanned the horizon for help, but none seemed forthcoming.

Exhausted, he eventually managed to build a "little hut" out of driftwood to protect him from the elements, and to store his few possessions. But then one day, after scavenging for food, he arrived home to find his little hut in flames, the smoke rolling up to the sky. The worst had happened; everything was lost. He was stunned with grief and anger. "God, how could you do this to me!" he cried.

Early the next day, however, he was awakened by the sound of a ship that was approaching the island. It had come to rescue him. "How did you know I was here?" asked the weary man of his rescuers. "We saw your smoke signal," they replied.

It is easy to get discouraged when things are going bad. But we shouldn't lose heart, because God is at work in our lives, even in the midst of pain and suffering. Remember, next time your little hut is burning to the ground" it just may be a smoke signal that summons the grace of God.

– *Author Unknown*

It's Your Move Daughter

I gave you life,
    but I cannot live it for you.
I can teach you things,
    but I cannot make you learn.

I can give you directions,
    but I cannot always be there to lead you.
I can allow you freedom,
    but cannot account for it.

I can take you to church,
    but cannot make you believe.
I can teach you right from wrong,
    but I can't always decide for you.

I can buy you beautiful clothes,
    but I cannot make you lovely inside.
I can offer you advice,
    but I cannot accept it for you.

I can give you love,
    but I cannot force it upon you.
I can teach you to be a friend,
    but I cannot make you one.

I can teach you to share,
    but I cannot make you unselfish.
I can teach you respect,
    but I can't force you to show honor.

I can grieve about your report card,
    but I cannot doubt your teachers.
I can advise you about friends,
    but I cannot choose them for you.

I can teach you about sex,
    but I cannot keep you pure.
I can tell you the facts of life,
    but I can't build your reputation.

I can tell you about drink,
    but I can't say NO for you.
I can warn you about drugs,
    but I can't prevent you from using them.

I can tell you about lofty goals,
    but I can't achieve them for you.
I can teach you kindness,
    but I can't force you to be gracious.

I can warn you about sins,
    but I cannot make your morals.
I can love you as a daughter,
    but I cannot place you in God's family.

I can pray for you,
    but I cannot make you walk with God.
I can teach you about Jesus,
    but I cannot make HIM your Saviour.

I can teach you to OBEY,
    but I cannot make Jesus your Lord.
I can tell you how to live,
    but I cannot give you Eternal Life.

Thanks for listening,
Dad and Mom
(SON can be inserted instead of DAUGHTER)

John Glenn Is a True Hero!

For half a century, the world has applauded John Glenn as a heart-stirring American hero. He lifted the nation's spirits when, as one of the original Mercury 7 astronauts, he was blasted alone into orbit around the Earth; the enduring affection for him is so powerful that even now people find themselves misting up at the sight of his face or the sound of his voice.

But for all these years, Glenn has had a hero of his own, someone who he has seen display endless courage of a different kind: her name is Annie Glenn.

They have been married for 69 years. (April 6, 1943)

He is 90. She is 92. (2012)

This weekend there has been news coverage of the 50th anniversary of Glenn's flight into orbit. We are being reminded that, half a century down the line, he remains America's unforgettable hero.

He has never really bought that.

Because the heroism he most cherishes is of a sort that is seldom cheered. It belongs to the person he has known longer than he has known anyone else in the world.

John Glenn and Annie Castor first knew each other when " literally" they shared a playpen.

In New Concord, Ohio, his parents and hers were friends. When the families got together, their children played.

John - the future Marine fighter pilot, the future test-pilot ace, the future astronaut was pure gold from the start. He would end up having what it took to rise to the absolute pinnacle of American regard during the space race; imagine what it meant to be the young John Glenn in the small confines of New Concord.

Three-sport varsity athlete, most admired boy in town, Mr. Everything.

Annie Castor was bright, was caring, was talented, was generous of spirit. But she could talk only with the most excruciating of difficulty. It haunted her.

Her stuttering was so severe that it was categorized as an 85% disability – 85% of the time, she could not manage to make words come out.

When she tried to recite a poem in elementary school, she was laughed at. She was not able to speak on the telephone. She could not have a regular conversation with a friend.

And John Glenn loved her.

Even as a boy he was wise enough to understand that people who could not see past her stutter were missing out on knowing a rare and wonderful girl.

They married on April 6, 1943. As a military wife, she found that life as she and John moved around the country could be quite hurtful. She has written: "I can remember some very painful experiences – especially the ridicule."

In department stores, she would wander unfamiliar aisles trying to find the right section, embarrassed to attempt to ask the salesclerks for help. In taxis, she would have to write requests to the driver, because she couldn't speak the destination out loud. In restaurants, she would point to the items on the menu.

A fine musician, Annie, in every community where she and John moved, would play the organ in church as a way to make new friends. She and John had two children. She has written: "Can you imagine living in the modern world and being afraid to use the telephone? 'Hello' used to be so hard for me to say. I worried that my children would be injured and need a doctor. Could I somehow find the words to get the information across on the phone?"

John, as a Marine aviator, flew 59 combat missions in World War II and 90 during the Korean War. Every time he was deployed, he and Annie said goodbye the same way. His last words to her before leaving were:

"I'm just going down to the corner store to get a pack of gum."

And, with just the two of them there, she was able to always reply:

"Don't be long."

On that February day in 1962 when the world held its breath and the Atlas rocket was about to propel him toward space, those were their words, once again. And in 1998, when, at 77, he went back to space aboard the shuttle Discovery, it was an understandably tense time for them. What if something happened to end their life together?

She knew what he would say to her before boarding the shuttle. He did – and this time he gave her a present to hold onto:

A pack of gum.

She carried it in a pocket next to her heart until he was safely home.

Many times in her life she attempted various treatments to cure her stutter. None worked.

But in 1973, she found a doctor in Virginia who ran an intensive program she and John hoped would help her. She traveled there to enroll and to give it her best effort. The miracle she and John had always waited for at last, as miracles will do, arrived. At age 53, she was able to talk fluidly, and not in brief, anxiety-ridden, agonizing bursts.

John has said that on the first day he heard her speak to him with confidence and clarity, he dropped to his knees to offer a prayer of gratitude.

He has written: "I saw Annie's perseverance and strength through the years and it just made me admire her and love her even more." He has heard roaring ovations in countries around the globe for his own valor, but his awe is reserved for Annie, and what she accomplished: "I don't know if I would have had the courage."

Her voice is so clear and steady now that she regularly gives public talks. If you are lucky enough to know the Glenns, the sight and sound of them bantering and joking with each other and playfully finishing each others' sentences is something that warms you and makes you thankful just to be in the same room.

February 20, 2012 was the 50t anniversary of the Mercury Space shot, and once again people will remember, and will speak of the heroism of Glenn the astronaut.

But if you ever find yourself at an event where the Glenns are appearing, and you want to see someone so brimming with pride and love that you may feel your own tears start to well up, wait until the moment that Annie stands to say a few words to the audience.

And as she begins, take a look at her husband's eyes.

Let's Run Through the Rain

She must have been 6 years old, this beautiful brown haired, freckled-faced image of innocence. Her Mom looked like someone from the Walton's or a moment captured by Norman Rockwell. Not that she was old-fashioned. Her brown hair was ear length with enough curl to appear natural. She had on a pair of tan shorts and light blue knit shirt. Her sneakers were white with a blue trim. She looked like a Mom.

It was pouring outside. The kind of rain that gushes over the tops of rain gutters, so much in a hurry to hit the earth it has no time to flow down the spout. Drains in the nearby parking lot were filled to capacity and some were blocked so that huge puddles made lakes around parked cars.

We all stood there under the awning and just inside the door of the Wal-Mart. We waited, some patiently, others irritated because nature messed up their hurried day.

I am always mesmerized by rain fall. I get lost in the sound and sight of the heavens washing away the dirt and dust of the world. Memories of running, splashing so carefree as a child came pouring in as a welcome reprieve from the worries of my day. Her voice was so sweet as it broke the hypnotic trance we were all caught in. "Mom, let's run through the rain," she said.

"What?" Mom asked.

"Let's run through the rain!" she repeated.

"No, honey. We'll wait until it slows down a bit," Mom replied.

This young child waited about another minute and repeated her statement.

"Mom. Let's run through the rain."

"We'll get soaked if we do," Mom said.

"No, we won't, Mom. That's not what you said this morning," the young girl said as she tugged at her Mom's arm.

"This morning? When did I say we could run through the rain and not get wet?"

"Don't you remember? When you were talking to Daddy about his cancer, you said, "If God can get us through this, He can get us through anything!"

The entire crowd stopped dead silent. I swear you couldn't hear anything but the rain. We all stood silently. No one came or left in the next few minutes. Mom paused and thought for a moment about what she would say.

Now some would laugh it off and scold her for being silly. Some might even ignore what was said. But this was a moment of affirmation in a young child's life. A time when innocent trust can be nurtured so that it will bloom into faith.

"Honey, you are absolutely right. Let's run through the rain. If God lets us get wet, well maybe we just needed washing," Mom said. Then off they ran. We all stood watching, smiling and laughing as they darted past the cars and yes through the puddles. They held their shopping bags over their heads just in case. They got soaked.

And they were followed by a few believers who screamed and laughed like children all the way to their cars. Perhaps inspired by their faith and trust. I want to believe that somewhere down the road in life, Mom will find herself reflecting back on moments they spent together, captured like pictures in the scrapbook of her cherished memories.

Maybe when she watches proudly as her daughter graduates. Or as her Daddy walks her down the aisle on her wedding day. She will laugh again. Her heart will beat a little faster. Her smile will tell the world they love each other.

But only two people will share that precious moment when they ran through the rain believing that God would get them through.

And Yes, I did. I ran. I got wet. I needed washing.

To everything there is a season and a time to every purpose under the heaven." Ecclesiastes 3:1

– *Author Unknown*

Not Home Yet

An old missionary couple had been working in Africa for years and was returning to New York to retire. They had no pension; their health was broken; they were defeated, discouraged, and afraid. They discovered they were booked on the same ship as President Teddy Roosevelt, who was returning from one of his big-game hunting expeditions.

No one paid any attention to them. They watched the fanfare that accompanied the President's entourage, with passengers trying to catch a glimpse of the great man. As the ship moved across the ocean, the old missionary said to his wife, "Something is wrong.

Why should we have given our lives in faithful service for God in Africa all these many years and have no one care a thing about us? Here this man comes back from a hunting trip and everybody makes much over him, but nobody gives two hoots about us."

"Dear, you shouldn't feel that way," his wife said.

"I can't help it; it doesn't seem right," he replied.

When the ship docked in New York, a band was waiting to greet the President. The mayor and other dignitaries were there. The papers were full of the President's arrival.

No one noticed this missionary couple. They slipped off the ship and found a cheap flat on the East Side, hoping the next day to see what they could do to make a living in the city.

That night the man's spirit broke. He said to his wife, "I can't take this; God is not treating us fairly." His wife replied, "Why don't you go in the bedroom and tell that to the Lord?"

A short time later he came out from the bedroom, but now his face was completely different. His wife asked, "Dear, what happened?"

"The Lord settled it with me," he said. "I told him how bitter I was that the President should receive this tremendous homecoming, when no one met us as we returned home. And when I finished, it seemed as though the Lord put His hand on my shoulder and simply said, "But you're not home yet!"

– *Author Unknown*

On Picking up Pennies

You always hear the usual stories of pennies on the sidewalk being good luck, gifts from angels, etc. This is the first time I've ever heard this twist on the story. Gives you something to think about.

Several years ago, a friend of mine and her husband were invited to spend the weekend at the husband's employer's home. My friend, Arlene, was nervous about the weekend. The boss was very wealthy, with a fine home on the waterway, and cars costing more than her house.

The first day and evening went well, and Arlene was delighted to have this rare glimpse into how the very wealthy live. The husband's employer was quite generous as a host, and took them to the finest restaurants. Arlene knew she would never have the opportunity to indulge in this kind of extravagance again, so was enjoying herself immensely.

As the three of them were about to enter an exclusive restaurant that evening, the boss was walking slightly ahead of Arlene and her husband. He stopped suddenly, looking down on the pavement for a long, silent moment.

Arlene wondered if she was supposed to pass him. There was nothing on the ground except a single darkened penny that someone had dropped, and a few cigarette butts.

Still silent, the man reached down and picked up the penny. He held it up and smiled, then put it in his pocket as if he had found a great treasure. How absurd! What need did this man have for a single penny? Why would he even take the time to stop and pick it up?

Throughout dinner, the entire scene nagged at her. Finally, she could stand it no longer. She casually mentioned that her daughter once had a coin collection, and asked if the penny he had found had been of some value.

A smile crept across the man's face as he reached into his pocket for the penny and held it out for her to see. She had seen many pennies before! What was the point of this?

'Look at it.' He said. 'Read what it says.' She read the words ' United States of America ' 'No, not that; read further.'

'One cent?'

'No, keep reading.'

'In God we Trust?' 'Yes!'

'And?'

'And if I trust in God, the name of God is holy, even on a coin. Whenever I find a coin I see that inscription. It is written on every single United States coin, but we never seem to notice it! God drops a message right in front of me telling me to trust Him? Who am I to pass it by? When I see a coin, I pray, I stop to see if my trust IS in God at that moment. I pick the coin up as a response to God; that I do trust in Him.

For a short time, at least, I cherished it as if it were gold. I think it is God's way of starting a conversation with me. Lucky for me, God is patient and pennies are plentiful!

When I was out shopping today, I found a penny on the sidewalk. I stopped and picked it up, and realized that I had been worrying and fretting in my mind about things I cannot change. I read the words, 'In God We Trust,' and had to laugh. Yes, God, I get the message.

It seems that I have been finding an inordinate number of pennies in the last few months, but then, pennies are plentiful!

And, God is patient.

Parable of the Pencil

The Pencil Maker took the pencil aside, just before putting him into the box. "There are 5 things you need to know," he told the pencil, "before I send you out into the world. Always remember them and never forget, and you will become the best pencil you can be.

One: You will be able to do many great things, but only if you allow yourself to be held in someone's hand.

Two: You will experience a painful sharpening from time to time, but you'll need it to become a better pencil.

Three: You will be able to correct mistakes you will make.

Four: The most important part of you will always be what's inside.

And Five: On every surface you are used on, you must leave your mark. No matter what the condition, you must continue to write."

The pencil understood and promised to remember, and went into the box with purpose in its heart.

Now replacing the place of the pencil with you; always remember them and never forget, and you will become the best person you can be.

One: You will be able to do many great things, but only if you allow yourself to be held in God's hand. And allow other human beings to access you for the many gifts you possess.

Two: You will experience a painful sharpening from time to time, by going through various problems, but you'll need it to become a stronger person.

Three: You will be able to correct mistakes you might make or grow through them.

Four: The most important part of you will always be what's on the inside.

And Five: On every surface you walk, you must leave your mark. No matter what the situation, you must continue to serve God in everything.

By understanding and remembering, let us proceed with our life on this earth having a meaningful purpose in our heart and a relationship with God daily.

– *Author Unknown*

Piano Concert

Wishing to encourage her young son's progress on the piano, a mother took her boy to a Paderewski concert. After they were seated, the mother spotted a friend in the audience and walked down the aisle to greet her.

Seizing the opportunity to explore the wonders of the concert hall, the little boy quietly got up and eventually explored his way through a door marked "NO ADMITTANCE."

When the house lights dimmed and the concert was about to begin, the mother returned to her seat and discovered that the child was missing. Suddenly, the curtains parted and spotlights focused on the impressive Steinway on stage.

In horror, the mother saw her little boy sitting at the keyboard, innocently picking out "Twinkle, Twinkle Little Star." At that moment, the great piano master made his entrance, quickly moved to the piano and whispered in the boy's ear, "Don't quit. Keep playing." Then leaning over, Paderewski reached down with his left hand and began filling in a bass part. Soon his right arm reached around to the other side of the child and he added a running obligato. Together, the old master and the young novice transformed a frightening situation into a wonderfully creative experience. The audience was mesmerized.

That's the way it is with God. What we can accomplish on our own is hardly noteworthy. We try our best, but the results aren't exactly graceful flowing music. But with the hand of the Master, our life's work truly can be beautiful.

The next time you set out to accomplish great feats, listen carefully. You can hear the voice of the Master, whispering in your ear, "Don't quit. Keep playing." Feel His loving arms around you. Know that His strong hands are there helping you turn your feeble attempts into true masterpieces.

Remember, God doesn't call the equipped, he equips the called. And He will always be there to love and guide you on to great things!

– *Author Unknown*

Playing for Mother

At the prodding of my friends I am writing this story. My name is Mildred Honor and I am a former elementary school music teacher from Des Moines, Iowa.

I have always supplemented my income by teaching piano lessons - something I have done for over 30 years. During those years I found that children have many levels of musical ability, and even though I have never had the pleasure of having a prodigy, I have taught some very talented students.

However, I have also had my share of what I call 'musically challenged' pupils - one such pupil being Robby. Robby was 11 years old when his mother (a single mom) dropped him off for his first piano lesson. I prefer that students (especially boys) begin at an earlier age, which I explained to Robby. But Robby said that it had always been his mother's dream to hear him play the piano, so I took him as a student.

Well, Robby began his piano lessons and from the beginning I thought it was a hopeless endeavor. As much as Robby tried, he lacked the sense of tone and basic rhythm needed to excel. But he dutifully reviewed his scales and some elementary piano pieces that I require all my students to learn. Over the months he tried and tried while I listened and cringed and tried to encourage him.

At the end of each weekly lesson he would always say 'My mom's going to hear me play someday'. But to me, it seemed hopeless, he just did not have any inborn ability.

I only knew his mother from a distance as she dropped Robby off or waited in her aged car to pick him up. She always waved and smiled, but never dropped in.

Then one day Robby stopped coming for his lessons. I thought about calling him, but assumed that because of his lack of ability he had decided to pursue something else. I was also glad that he had stopped coming - he was a bad advertisement for my teaching!

Several weeks later I mailed a flyer recital to the students' homes. To my surprise, Robby (who had received a flyer) asked me if he could be in the recital. I told him that the recital was for current pupils and that because he had dropped out, he really did not qualify.

He told me that his mother had been sick and unable to take him to his piano lessons, but that he had been practicing. "Please Miss Honor, I've just got to play," he insisted. I don't know what led me to allow him to play in the recital - perhaps it was his insistence or maybe something inside of me saying that it would be all right.

The night of the recital came and the high school gymnasium was packed with parents, relatives and friends. I put Robby last in the program, just before I was to come up and thank all the students and play a finishing piece. I thought that any damage he might do would come at the end of the program and I could always salvage his poor performance through my 'curtain closer'.

Well, the recital went off without a hitch, the students had been practicing and it showed. Then Robby came up on the stage. His clothes were wrinkled and his hair looked as though he had run an egg beater through it. 'Why wasn't he dressed up like the other students?' I thought. 'Why didn't his mother at least make him comb his hair for this special night?'

Robby pulled out the piano bench, and I was surprised when he announced that he had chosen to play Mozart's Concerto No. 21 in C Major. I was not prepared for what I heard next. His fingers were light on the keys, they even danced nimbly on the ivories. He went from pianissimo to fortissimo, from allegro to virtuoso; his suspended chords that Mozart demands were magnificent!

Never had I heard Mozart played so well by anyone his age. After six and a half minutes he ended in a grand crescendo, and everyone was on their feet in wild applause! Overcome and in tears, I ran up onstage and put my arms around Robby in joy. 'I have never heard you play like that Robby, how did you do it?

Through the microphone Robby explained: "Well, Miss Honor, remember I told you that my mom was sick? Well, she actually had cancer and passed away this morning. And well . . . she was born deaf, so tonight was the first time she had ever heard me play, and I wanted to make it special."

There wasn't a dry eye in the house that evening. As the people from Social Services led Robby from the stage to be placed into foster care, I noticed that even their eyes were red and puffy. I thought to myself then how much richer my life had been for taking Robby as my pupil.

No, I have never had a prodigy, but that night I became a prodigy – of Robby. He was the teacher and I was the pupil, for he had taught me the meaning of perseverance and love and believing in yourself, and may be even taking a chance on someone and you didn't know why.

Robby was killed years later in the senseless bombing of the Alfred P.

Murray Federal Building in Oklahoma City in April, 1995.

And now, a footnote to the story. If you are thinking about sharing this message, you are probably wondering which friends aren't the 'appropriate' ones to receive this type of message. This was included in this book because the compiler believes that we can all make a difference!

So many seemingly trivial interactions between two people present us with a choice:

Do we act with compassion or do we pass up that opportunity and leave the world a bit colder in the process?

If God didn't have a purpose for us, we wouldn't be here!

IN GOD WE TRUST!

Five Steps for Living

Live simply.

Love generously.

Care deeply.

Speak kindly.

Leave the rest to God

Praying for Ice Cream

Last week, I took my grand-children to a restaurant. My six-year-old grand-son asked if he could say grace.

As we bowed our heads he said, "God is good, God is great. Thank you for the food, and I would even thank you more if Nana gets us ice cream for dessert. And liberty and justice for all! Amen!"

Along with the laughter from the other customers nearby, I heard a woman remark, "That's what's wrong with this country. Kids today don't even know how to pray. Asking God for ice cream! Why, I never!"

Hearing this, my grand-son burst into tears and asked me, "Did I do it wrong? Is God mad at me?"

As I held him and assured him that he had done a terrific job, and God was certainly not mad at him, an elderly gentleman approached the table.

He winked at my grand-son and said, "I happen to know that God thought that was a great prayer."

"Really?" my grand-son asked.

"Cross my heart," the man replied.

Then, in a theatrical whisper, he added (indicating the woman whose remark had started this whole thing), "Too bad she never asks God for ice cream. A little ice cream is good for the soul sometimes."

Naturally, I bought my grand-children ice cream at the end of the meal. My grand-son stared at his for a moment, and then did something I will remember the rest of my life.

He picked up his sundae and, without a word, walked over and placed it in front of the woman. With a big smile he told her, "Here, this is for you. Ice cream is good for the soul sometimes; and my soul is good already."

Puppies for Sale

A farmer had some puppies he needed to sell. He painted a sign advertising the 4 pups and set about nailing it to a post on the edge of his yard. As he was driving the last nail into the post, he felt a tug on his overalls. He looked down into the eyes of a little boy.

"Mister," he said, "I want to buy one of your puppies." "Well," said the farmer, as he rubbed the sweat off the back of his neck, "These puppies come from fine parents and cost a good deal of money."

The boy dropped his head for a moment. Then reaching deep into his pocket, he pulled out a handful of change and held it up to the farmer.

"I've got thirty-nine cents. Is that enough to take a look?"

"Sure," said the farmer. And with that he let out a whistle. "Here, Dolly!" he called.

Out from the doghouse and down the ramp ran Dolly followed by four little balls of fur.

The little boy pressed his face against the chain link fence. His eyes danced with delight. As the dogs made their way to the fence, the little boy noticed something else stirring inside the doghouse.

Slowly another little ball appeared, this one noticeably smaller. Down the ramp it slid. Then in a somewhat awkward manner, the little pup began hobbling toward the others, doing its best to catch up.

"I want that one," the little boy said, pointing to the runt. The farmer knelt down at the boy's side and said, "Son, you don't want that puppy. He will never be able to run and play with you like these other dogs would."

With that the little boy stepped back from the fence, reached down, and began rolling up one leg of his trousers.

In doing so he revealed a steel brace running down both sides of his leg attaching itself to a specially made shoe.

Looking back up at the farmer, he said, "You see sir, I don't run too well myself, and he will need someone who understands."

With tears in his eyes, the farmer reached down and picked up the little pup.

Holding it carefully he handed it to the little boy. "How much?" asked the little boy. "No charge," answered the farmer, "There's no charge for love."

The world is full of people who need someone who understands.

R-Rated Cookies

A boy came home and asked his Mother if he could go to a show that was R rated. His Mother said, "No, there is to much profanity in it." He replied, "But Mother I can handle it and besides there is not much, just a little bit." But the Mother still said "No" and he pouted the rest of the evening.

The next day, when he came home from school, with a couple of his buddies, there was a plate of his favorite cookies his Mother had baked. He said to his buddies. "Mother regrets she did not let me go to that movie and is trying to make up for it."

Just as the boys reached for a cookie his mother said, "Oh, I must tell you, I put some dog doo in the cookies. Not much. Just a little but you are able to handle it – kind of like that little bit of bad in the movie you wanted to see."

Reflection on Children

"One of these days you'll shout, "Why don't you kids grow up and act your age!" And they will. Or you'll say, "Kids, get outside and find yourselves something to do . . . and don't slam the door!" And they won't. You'll straighten the boys' bedrooms neat and tidy . . . bumper stickers discarded . . . spread tucked and smooth . . . toys displayed on the shelves. Hangers in the closet with clothes attached. Animals caged. And you'll say out loud, "Now I want it to stay just like this!" And it will. You'll prepare a perfect dinner with a salad that hasn't been picked to death and a cake with no finger traces in the icing, and you'll say, "Now there's a meal for company!" And you'll eat it alone. You'll say, "I want complete privacy on the phone. No dancing around. No pantomimes. No demolition crews. Silence! Do you hear?" And you'll have it. No more plastic place mats stained with spaghetti. No more spreads to protect sofas from damp bottoms and dusty shoes. No more gates to stumble over in the doorway of the baby's room. No more hot wheels or Barbie dolls under the couch. No more playpens to arrange a room around.

No more anxious nights under a vaporizer tent. No more cracker crumbs on the sheets. No more wall-to-wall water in the bathroom. No more iron-on patches. No wet, knotted shoelaces, pants with knees out, or rubber bands for pony tails. Imagine, a lipstick with a point on it. Not having to get a babysitter on New Year's Eve.

Family washing only once a week. Seeing a steak that isn't ground. Marketing with only groceries in the basket. No PTA meetings. No more car pools. No blaring radios or Sesame Street three times a day on the television. No more washing her hair at 9 o'clock at night . . . and no more wondering where is the family car? Having your own roll of Scotch Tape. Think about it. No more Christmas presents out of construction paper and will-hold glue. No more sloppy oatmeal kisses. No more tooth fairy. No more giggles in the dark. No knees to heal; no responsibility. Only a voice *crying*, "Why don't you grow up!" And the silence echoing, "I did!"

– *Author Unknown*

Service Men's Lunches

I put my carry-on in the luggage compartment and sat down in my assigned seat. It was going to be a long flight. "I'm glad I have a good book to read. Perhaps I will get a short nap," I thought.

Just before take-off, a line of soldiers came down the aisle and filled all the vacant seats, totally surrounding me. I decided to start a conversation.

"Where are you headed?' I asked the soldier seated nearest to me. "Petawawa. We'll be there for two weeks for special training, and then we're being deployed to Afghanistan."

After flying for about an hour, an announcement was made that sack lunches were available for five dollars. It would be several hours before we reached the east, and I quickly decided a lunch would help pass the time.

As I reached for my wallet, I overheard a soldier ask his buddy if he planned to buy lunch. "No, that seems like a lot of money for just a sack lunch," he replied. "Probably wouldn't be worth five bucks. I'll wait till we get to base."

His friend agreed.

I looked around at the other soldiers. None were buying lunch. I walked to the back of the plane and handed the flight attendant a fifty dollar bill. 'Take a lunch to all those soldiers.' She grabbed my arms and squeezed tightly. Her eyes wet with tears, she thanked me. "My son was a soldier in Iraq; it's almost like you are doing it for him," she said.

Picking up ten sacks, she headed up the aisle to where the soldiers were seated. She stopped at my seat and asked, "Which do you like best - beef or Chicken?" "Chicken," I replied, wondering why she asked. She turned and went to the front of plane, returning a minute later with a dinner plate from first class. "This is your thanks."

After we finished eating, I went again to the back of the plane, heading for the rest room. A man stopped me. "I saw what you did. I want to be part of it. Here, take this." He handed me twenty-five dollars.

Soon after I returned to my seat, I saw the Flight Captain coming down the aisle, looking at the aisle number as he walked, I hoped he was not looking for me, but noticed he was looking at the numbers only on my side of the plane.

When he got to my row he stopped, smiled, held out his hand and said, "I want to shake your hand." Quickly unfastening my seatbelt I stood and took the Captain's hand. With a booming voice he said, 'I was a soldier and

I was a military pilot. Once, someone bought me a lunch. It was an act of kindness I never forgot." I was embarrassed when applause was heard from all of the passengers.

Later I walked to the front of the plane so I could stretch my legs. A man who was seated about six rows in front of me reached out his hand, wanting to shake mine. He left another twenty-five dollars in my palm.

When we landed I gathered my belongings and started to deplane. Waiting just inside the airplane door was a man who stopped me, put something in my shirt pocket, turned, and walked away without saying a word. Another twenty-five dollars!

Upon entering the Terminal, I saw the soldiers gathering for their trip to the base. I walked over to them and handed them the seventy-five dollars. "It will take you some time to reach the base. It will be about time for a sandwich. God Bless You.'

Ten young men left that flight feeling the love and respect of their fellow travelers.

As I walked briskly to my car, I whispered a prayer for their safe return. All service persons were giving their all for our country. A couple of meals. It seemed so little.

A veteran is someone who, at one point in his life, wrote a blank check made payable to 'The United States of America "for an amount of up to and including my life."

Shoes in Church

My alarm went off
It was Sunday again.
I was sleepy and tired
My one day to sleep in.
But the guilt I would feel
The rest of the day
Would have been too much
So I'd go and I'd pray.

I showered and shaved.
I adjusted my tie.
I got there and sat
In a pew just in time.
Bowing my head in prayer
As I closed my eyes.
I saw the shoe of the man next to me
Touching my own. I sighed.

With plenty of room on either side.
I thought, 'Why must our soles touch?'
It bothered me, his shoe touching mine
But it didn't bother him much.
A prayer began: 'Our Father'
I thought, 'This man with the shoes, has no pride.
They're dusty, worn, and scratched.
Even worse, there are holes on the side!'

'Thank You for blessings,' the prayer went on.
The shoe man said
A quiet 'Amen.'
I tried to focus on the prayer
But my thoughts were on his shoes again.
Aren't we supposed to look our best.
When walking through that door?
'Well, this certainly isn't it,' I thought,

Glancing toward the floor.
Then the prayer was ended
And the songs of praise began.
The shoe man was certainly loud
Sounding proud as he sang.
His voice lifted the rafters
His hands were raised high.
The Lord could surely hear.

The shoe man's voice from the sky.
It was time for the offering
And what I threw in was steep.
I watched as the shoe man reached
Into his pockets so deep.
I saw what was pulled out
What the shoe man put in.
Then I heard a soft 'clink'

As when silver hits tin.
The sermon really bored me
To tears, and that's no lie.
It was the same for the shoe man.
For tears fell from his eyes.
At the end of the service
As is the custom here.
We must greet new visitors
And show them all good cheer.

But I felt moved somehow
And wanted to meet the shoe man.
So after the closing prayer
I reached over and shook his hand.
He was old and his skin was dark
And his hair was truly a mess.
But I thanked him for coming
For being our guest.

He said, 'My names' Charlie
I'm glad to meet you, my friend.'
There were tears in his eyes
But he had a large, wide grin.

'Let me explain,' he said
Wiping tears from his eyes.
'I've been coming here for months
And you're the first to say 'Hi.''

'I know that my appearance'
Is not like all the rest.
'But I really do try
To always look my best.'
'I always clean and polish my shoes,
before my very long walk.
'But by the time I get here
'They're dirty and dusty, like chalk.'

My heart filled with pain.
And I swallowed to hide my tears.
As he continued to apologize
For daring to sit so near
He said, 'When I get here
'I know I must look a sight.
'But I thought if I could touch you.
'Then maybe our souls might unite.'

I was silent for a moment
Knowing whatever was said
Would pale in comparison.
I spoke from my heart, not my head.
'Oh, you've touched me,' I said
And taught me, in part;
'That the best of any man
'Is what is found in his heart.'

The rest, I thought,
This shoe man will never know.
Like just how thankful I really am
That his dirty old shoe touched my soul.

Spilled Books and Suicide

One day, when I was a freshman in high school, I saw a kid from my class was walking home from school alone. His name was Kyle. It looked like he was carrying all of his books. I thought to myself, "Why would anyone bring home all his books on a Friday? He must really be a nerd." I had quite a weekend planned (parties and a football game with my friends tomorrow afternoon), so I shrugged my shoulders and went on.

As I was walking, I saw a bunch of kids running toward him. They ran at him, knocking all his books out of his arms and tripping him so he landed in the dirt. His glasses went flying, and I saw them land in the grass about ten feet from him. He looked up and I saw this terrible sadness in his eyes. My heart went out to him. So, I jogged over to him and as he crawled around looking for his glasses, and I saw a tear in his eye.

As I handed him his glasses, I said, "Those guys are jerks. They really should get lives." He looked at me and said, "Hey thanks!" There was a big smile on his face. It was one of those smiles that showed real gratitude. I helped him pick up his books, and asked him where he lived. As it turned out, he lived near me, so I asked him why I had never seen him before. He said he had gone to private school before now.

I would have never hung out with a private school kid before. We talked all the way home, and I carried his books. He turned out to be a pretty cool kid. I asked him if he wanted to play football on Saturday with me and my friends. He said yes. We hung all weekend and the more I got to know Kyle, the more I liked him. And my friends thought the same of him. Monday morning came, and there was Kyle with the huge stack of books again. I stopped him and said, "Boy, you are gonna really build some serious muscles with this pile of books everyday!" He just laughed and handed me half the books.

Over the next four years, Kyle and I became best friends. When we were seniors, began to think about college. Kyle decided on Georgetown, and I was going to Duke. I knew that we would always be friends, that the miles would never be a problem. He was going to be a doctor, and I was going for business on a football scholarship. Kyle was valedictorian of our class. I teased him all the time about being a nerd. He had to prepare a speech for graduation. I was so glad it wasn't me having to get up there and speak.

Graduation day, I saw Kyle. He looked great. He was one of those guys that really found himself during high school. He filled out and actually looked good in glasses. He had more dates than me and all the girls loved him! Boy, sometimes I was jealous. Today was one of those days. I could see that he was nervous about his speech. So, I smacked him on the back and said, "Hey, big guy, you'll be great!" He looked at me with one of those looks (the really grateful one) and smiled. "Thanks," he said.

As he started his speech, he cleared his throat, and began: "Graduation is a time to thank those who helped you make it through those tough years. Your parents, your teachers, your siblings, maybe a coach . . . but mostly your friends. I am here to tell all of you that being a friend to someone is the best gift you can give them. I am going to tell you a story." I just looked at my friend with disbelief as he told the story of the first day we met. He had planned to kill himself over the weekend. He talked of how he had cleaned out his locker so his mom wouldn't have to do it later and was carrying his stuff home. He looked hard at me and gave me a little smile. "Thankfully, I was saved. My friend saved me from doing the unspeakable." I heard the gasp go through the crowd as this handsome, popular boy told us all about his weakest moment. I saw his mom and dad looking at me smiling that same grateful smile. Not until that moment did I realize it's depth.

Never underestimate the power of your actions. With one small gesture you can change a person's life. For better or for worse. God puts us all in each other's lives to impact one another in some way.

Thanks for Your Time

A young man learns what's most important in life from the guy next door. It had been some time since Jack had seen the old man. College, girls, career, and life itself got in the way. In fact, Jack moved clear across the country in pursuit of his dreams. There, in the rush of his busy life, Jack had little time to think about the past and often no time to spend with his wife and son. He was working on his future, and nothing could stop him. Over the phone, his mother told him, "Mr. Belser died last night. The funeral is Wednesday." Memories flashed through his mind like an old newsreel as he sat quietly remembering his childhood days.

"Jack, did you hear me?" "Oh, sorry, Mom. Yes, I heard you. It's been so long since I thought of him. I'm sorry, but I honestly thought he died years ago," Jack said.

"Well, he didn't forget you. Every time I saw him he'd ask how you were doing. He'd reminisce about the many days you spent over 'his side of the fence' as he put it," Mom told him.

"I loved that old house he lived in," Jack said.

"You know, Jack, after your father died, Mr. Belser stepped in to make sure you had a man's influence in your life," she said.

"He's the one who taught me carpentry," he said. "I wouldn't be in this business if it weren't for him. He spent a lot of time teaching me things he thought were important. Mom, I'll be there for the funeral," Jack said.

As busy as he was, he kept his word. Jack caught the next flight to his hometown. Mr. Belser's funeral was small and uneventful. He had no children of his own, and most of his relatives had passed away.The night before he had to return home, Jack and his Mom stopped by to see the old house next door one more time. Standing in the doorway, Jack paused for a moment. It was like crossing over into another dimension, a leap through space and time. The house was exactly as he remembered. Every step held memories. Every picture, every piece of furniture. Jack stopped suddenly.

"What's wrong, Jack?" his Mom asked.

"The box is gone," he said

"What box?" Mom asked.

"There was a small gold box that he kept locked on top of his desk. I must have asked him a thousand times what was inside. All he'd ever tell me was 'the thing I value most,'" Jack said.

It was gone. Everything about the house was exactly how Jack remembered it, except for the box. He figured someone from the Belser family had taken it.

"Now I'll never know what was so valuable to him," Jack said. "I better get some sleep. I have an early flight home, Mom."

It had been about two weeks since Mr. Belser died. Returning home from work one day Jack discovered a note in his mailbox. "Signature required on a package. No one at home. Please stop by the main post office within the next three days," the note read.

Early the next day Jack retrieved the package. The small box was old and looked like it had been mailed a hundred years ago. The handwriting was difficult to read, but the return address caught his attention. "Mr. Harold Belser" it read. Jack took the box out to his car and ripped open the package. There inside was the gold box and an envelope.

Jack's hands shook as he read the note inside."Upon my death, please forward this box and its contents to Jack Bennett. It's the thing I valued most in my life." A small key was taped to the letter. His heart racing, as tears filling his eyes, Jack carefully unlocked the box. There inside he found a beautiful gold pocket watch.

Running his fingers slowly over the finely etched casing, he unlatched the cover. Inside he found these words engraved:

"Jack, Thanks for your time! -Harold Belser."

"The thing he valued most was. . . my time".

Jack held the watch for a few minutes, then called his office and cleared his appointments for the next two days.

"Why?" Janet, his assistant asked.

"I need some time to spend with my son," he said."Oh, by the way, Janet, thanks for your time!"

Life is not measured by the number of breaths we take but by the moments that take our breath away.

The Cab Ride

I arrived at the address and honked the horn. After waiting a few minutes I walked to the door and knocked. "Just a minute," answered a frail, elderly voice. I could hear something being dragged across the floor.

After a long pause, the door opened. A small woman in her 90's stood before me. She was wearing a print dress and a pillbox hat with a veil pinned on it, like somebody out of a 1940's movie.

By her side was a small nylon suitcase. The apartment looked as if no one had lived in it for years. All the furniture was covered with sheets. There were no clocks on the walls, no knickknacks or utensils on the counters. In the corner was a cardboard box filled with photos and glassware.

"Would you carry my bag out to the car?" she said. I took the suitcase to the cab, then returned to assist the woman. She took my arm and we walked slowly toward the curb.

She kept thanking me for my kindness. "It's nothing", I told her. "I just try to treat my passengers the way I would want my mother treated".

"Oh, you're such a good boy", she said. When we got in the cab, she gave me an address and then asked, "Could you drive through downtown?"

"It's not the shortest way," I answered quickly.

"Oh, I don't mind," she said. I'm in no hurry. I'm on my way to a hospice."

I looked in the rear-view mirror. Her eyes were glistening. "I don't have any family left," she continued in soft voice. "The doctor says I don't have very long." I quietly reached over and shut off the meter.

"What route would you like me to take?" I asked.

For the next two hours, we drove through the city. She showed me the building where she had once worked as an elevator operator.

We drove through the neighborhood where she and her husband had lived when they were newlyweds. She had me pull up in front of a furniture warehouse that had once been a ballroom where she had gone dancing as a girl. Sometimes she'd ask me to slow in front of a particular building or corner and would sit staring into the darkness, saying nothing.

As the first hint of sun was creasing the horizon, she suddenly said,

"I'm tired. Let's go now."

We drove in silence to the address she had given me. It was a low building, like a small convalescent home, with a driveway that passed under a portico.

Two orderlies came out to the cab as soon as we pulled up. They were solicitous and intent, watching her every move. They must have been expecting her.

I opened the trunk and took the small suitcase to the door. The woman was already seated in a wheelchair. "How much do I owe you?" she asked, reaching into her purse.

"Nothing," I said.

"You have to make a living," she answered.

"There are other passengers," I responded.

Almost without thinking, I bent and gave her a hug. She held onto me tightly.

"You gave an old woman a little moment of joy," she said. "Thank you."

I squeezed her hand, and they walked into the dim morning light. Behind me, a door shut. It was the sound of the closing of a life.

I didn't pick up any more passengers that shift. I drove aimlessly lost in thought. For the rest of that day, I could hardly talk. What if that woman had gotten an angry driver, or one who was impatient to end his shift? What if I had refused to take the run, or had honked once, then driven away?

On a quick review, I don't think that I have done anything differently.

We're conditioned to think that our lives revolve around great moments. But great moments often catch ununaware- beautifully wrapped in what others may consider a small one.

PEOPLE MAY NOT REMEMBER EXACTLY WHAT YOU DID, OR WHAT YOU SAID ~BUT~THEY WILL ALWAYS REMEMBER HOW YOU MADE THEM FEEL.

The Daffodil Principal

Several times my daughter had telephoned to say, "Mother, you must come to see the daffodils before they are over."

I wanted to go, but it was a two-hour drive from Laguna to Lake Arrowhead "I will come next Tuesday", I promised a little reluctantly on her third call.

Next Tuesday dawned, cold and rainy. Still, I had promised, and reluctantly I drove there. When I finally walked into Carolyn's house I was welcomed by the joyful sounds of happy children. I delightedly hugged and greeted my grandchildren.

"Forget the daffodils, Carolyn! The road is invisible in these clouds and fog, and there is nothing in the world except you and these children that I want to see badly enough to drive another inch!"

My daughter smiled calmly and said, "We drive in this all the time, Mother."

"Well, you won't get me back on the road until it clears, and then I'm heading for home!" I assured her.

"But first we're going to see the daffodils. It's just a few blocks," Carolyn said. "I'll drive. I'm used to this."

"Carolyn," I said sternly, "Please turn around."

"It's all right, Mother, I promise. You will never forgive yourself if you miss this experience."

After about twenty minutes, we turned onto a small gravel road and I saw a small church. On the far side of the church, I saw a hand lettered sign with an arrow that read, "Daffodil Garden." We got out of the car, each took a child's hand, and I followed Carolyn down the path. Then, as we turned a corner, I looked up and gasped. Before me lay the most glorious sight.

It looked as though someone had taken a great vat of gold and poured it over the mountain peak and its surrounding slopes. The flowers were planted in majestic, swirling patterns, great ribbons and swaths of deep orange, creamy white, lemon yellow, salmon pink, and saffron and butter yellow. Each different-colored variety was planted in large groups so that it swirled and flowed like its own river with its own unique hue. There were five acres of flowers.

"Who did this?" I asked Carolyn.

"Just one woman," Carolyn answered. "She lives on the property. That's her home." Carolyn pointed to a well-kept A-frame house, small and modestly sitting in the midst of all that glory. We walked up to the house.

On the patio, we saw a poster. "**Answers to the Questions I Know You Are Asking**", was the headline. The first answer was a simple one. "50,000 bulbs," it read. The second answer was, "One at a time, by one woman. Two hands, two feet, and one brain." The third answer was, "Began in 1958."

For me, that moment was a life-changing experience. I thought of this woman whom I had never met, who, more than forty years before, had begun, one bulb at a time, to bring her vision of beauty and joy to an obscure mountaintop. Planting one bulb at a time, year after year, this unknown woman had forever changed the world in which she lived.

One day at a time, she had created something of extraordinary magnificence, beauty, and inspiration. The principle her daffodil garden taught is one of the greatest principles of celebration.

That is, learning to move toward our goals and desires one step at a time - often just one baby-step at time - and learning to love the doing, learning to use the accumulation of time. When we multiply tiny pieces of time with small increments of daily effort, we, too, will find we can accomplish magnificent things. We can change the world.

"It makes me sad in a way," I admitted to Carolyn. "What might I have accomplished if I had thought of a wonderful goal thirty-five or forty years ago and had worked away at it 'one bulb at a time' through all those years? Just think what I might have been able to achieve!"

My daughter summed up the message of the day in her usual direct way. "Start tomorrow," she said.

She was right. It's so pointless to think of the lost hours of yesterdays. The way to make learning a lesson of celebration instead of a cause for regret is to only ask, "How can I put this to use today?"

Use the Daffodil Principle.

Stop waiting . . .

> Until your car or home is paid off
> Until you get a new car or home
> Until your kids leave the house
> Until you go back to school
> Until you finish school
> Until you clean the house
> Until you organize the garage
> Until you clean off your desk

Until you lose 10 lbs.

Until you gain 10 lbs.

Until you get married

Until you get a divorce

Until you have kids

Until the kids go to school

Until you retire

Until summer

Until spring

Until winter

Until fall

Until you die.

There is no better time than right now to be happy. Happiness is a journey, not a destination. So Work like you don't need money. Love like you've never been hurt, and, Dance like no one's watching.

The Dog's Name Is Lucky

Mary and her husband Jim had a dog. His name was Lucky and he was a real character. Whenever Mary and Jim had company come for a weekend visit they would warn their friends to not leave their luggage open because Lucky would help himself to whatever struck his fancy. Inevitably someone would forget and something would come up missing. Mary or Jim would go to Lucky's toy box in the basement and there the treasure would be, amid all of Lucky's favorite toys. Lucky always stashed his finds in his toy box and he was very particular that his toys stay in the box.

It happened that Mary found out she had breast cancer. Something told her she was going to die of this disease, she was just sure it was fatal. She scheduled the double mastectomy, fear riding her shoulders.

The night before she was to go to the hospital she cuddled with Lucky. A thought struck her... what would happen to Lucky? Although the three-year-old dog liked Jim he was Mary's dog through and through. If I die Lucky will be abandoned, Mary thought. He won't understand that I didn't want to leave him. The thought made her sadder than thinking of her own death.

The double mastectomy was harder on Mary than her doctors had anticipated and Mary was hospitalized for over two weeks. Jim took Lucky for his evening walk faithfully but the dog just drooped, whining and miserable. But finally the day came for Mary to leave the hospital. When she arrived home, Mary was so exhausted she couldn't even make it up the steps to her bedroom. Jim made his wife comfortable on the couch and left her to nap. Lucky stood watching Mary but he didn't come to her when she called. It made Mary sad but sleep soon overcame her and she dozed. When Mary woke for a second she couldn't understand what was wrong. She couldn't move her head and her body felt heavy and hot. Panic soon gave way to laughter though when Mary realized the problem. She was covered, literally blanketed in every treasure Lucky owned! While she had slept the sorrowing dog had made trip after trip to the basement and back bringing his beloved mistress his favorite things in life. He had covered her with his love. Mary forgot about dying. Instead she and Lucky began living again, walking further and further together every night.

It's been 12 years now and Mary is still cancer-free. Lucky? He still steals treasures and stashes them in his toy box but Mary remains his greatest treasure.

Live every day to the fullest . . . because every day is a blessing from God! He covers you with His treasures and His love!

The Funeral

Consumed by my loss, I didn't notice the hardness of the pew where I sat. I was at the funeral of my dearest friend - my mother. She finally had lost her long battle with cancer. The hurt was so intense; I found it hard to breathe at times. Always supportive, Mother clapped loudest at my school plays, held box of tissues while listening to my first heartbreak, comforted me at my father's death, encouraged me in college, and prayed for me my entire life. When mother's illness was diagnosed, my sister had a new baby and my brother had recently married his childhood sweetheart, so it fell on me, the 27-year-old middle child without entanglements, to take care of her. I counted it an honor.

'What now, Lord?' I asked sitting in the church. My life stretched out before me as an empty abyss. My brother sat stoically with his face toward the cross while clutching his wife's hand. My sister sat slumped against her husband's shoulder, his arms around her as she cradled their child–all so deeply grieving, no one noticed I sat alone.

My place had been with our mother, preparing her meals, helping her walk, taking her to the doctor, seeing to her medication, reading the Bible together. Now she was with the Lord. My work was finished, and I was alone.

At that moment, I heard a door open and slam shut at the back of the church. Quick footsteps hurried along the carpeted floor. An exasperated young man looked around briefly and then sat next to me. He folded his hands and placed them on his lap. His eyes were brimming with tears. He began to sniffle. "I'm late," he explained, though no explanation was necessary. After several eulogies, he leaned over and commented, "Why do they keep calling Mary by the name of ' Margaret?'" I said 'Because, that was her name, Margaret. Never Mary, no one called her 'Mary," I whispered.

I wondered why this person couldn't have sat on the other side of the church. He interrupted my grieving with his tears and fidgeting. Who was this stranger anyway?

"No, that isn't correct, he insisted, as several people glanced over at us whispering, "Her name is Mary, Mary Peters." "That isn't who this is."

"Isn't this the Lutheran church?" "No, the Lutheran church is across the street." "Oh, I believe you're at the wrong funeral, Sir."

The solemn moment of the occasion mixed with the realization of the man's mistake bubbled up inside me and came out as laughter. I cupped my hands over my face, hoping it would be interpreted as sobs. The creaking pew gave me away. Sharp looks from other mourners only made the situation seem more hilarious.

I peeked at the bewildered, misguided man seated beside me. He was laughing too, as he glanced around, deciding it was too late for an uneventful exit. I imagined Mother laughing. At the final 'Amen,' we darted out a door and into the parking lot. "I do believe we'll be the talk of the town," he laughed. He said his name was Rick and since he had missed his aunt's funeral, asked me out for a cup of coffee.

That afternoon began a lifelong journey for me with this man who attended the wrong funeral, but was in the right place. A year after our meeting, we were married at a country church where he was the assistant pastor. This time we both arrived at the same church, right on time.

In my time of sorrow, God gave me laughter. In place of loneliness, God gave me love. This past June, we celebrated our twenty-second wedding anniversary. Whenever anyone asks us how we met, Rick tells them, "Her mother and my Aunt Mary introduced us, and it's truly a match made in heaven."

The Necklace

The cheerful little girl with bouncy golden curls was almost five. Waiting with her mother at the checkout stand, she saw them, a circle of glistening white pearls in a pink foil box.

"Oh mommy please, Mommy. Can I have them? Please, Mommy, please?"

Quickly the mother checked the back of the little foil box and then looked back into the pleading blue eyes of her little girl's upturned face.

"A dollar ninety-five. That's almost $2.00. If you really want them, I'll think of some extra chores for you and in no time you can save enough money to buy them for yourself. Your birthday's only a week away and you might get another crisp dollar bill from Grandma."

As soon as Jenny got home, she emptied her penny bank and counted out 17 pennies. After dinner, she did more than her share of chores and she went to the neighbor and asked Mrs. McJames if she could pick dandelions for ten cents. On her birthday, Grandma did give her another new dollar bill and at last she had enough money to buy the necklace.

Jenny loved her pearls. They made her feel dressed up and grown up. She wore them everywhere, Sunday school, kindergarten, even to bed. The only time she took them off was when she went swimming or had a bubble bath. Mother said if they got wet, they might turn her neck green.

Jenny had a very loving daddy and every night when she was ready for bed, he would stop whatever he was doing and come upstairs to read her a story. One night as he finished the story, he asked Jenny, "Do you love me?"

"Oh yes, daddy. You know that I love you."

"Then give me your pearls."

"Oh, daddy, not my pearls. But you can have Princess, the white horse from my collection, the one with the pink tail. Remember, daddy? The one you gave me. She's my very favorite."

"That's okay, Honey, daddy loves you. Good night." And he brushed her cheek with a kiss.

About a week later, after the story time, Jenny's daddy asked again, "Do you love me?"

"Daddy, you know I love you." "Then give me your pearls."

"Oh Daddy, not my pearls. But you can have my baby doll. The brand

97

new one I got for my birthday. She is beautiful and you can have the yellow blanket that matches her sleeper."

"That's okay. Sleep well. God bless you, little one. Daddy loves you."

And as always, he brushed her cheek with a gentle kiss.

A few nights later when her daddy came in, Jenny was sitting on her bed with her legs crossed Indian style.

As he came close, he noticed her chin was trembling and one silent tear rolled down her cheek.

"What is it, Jenny? What's the matter?"

Jenny didn't say anything but lifted her little hand up to her daddy. And when she opened it, there was her little pearl necklace. With a little quiver, she finally said, "Here, daddy; this is for you."

With tears gathering in his own eyes, Jenny's daddy reached out with one hand to take the dime store necklace, and with the other hand he reached into his pocket and pulled out a blue velvet case with a strand of genuine pearls and gave them to Jenny.

He had them all the time. He was just waiting for her to give up the dime-store stuff so he could give her the genuine treasure.

So it is, with our Heavenly Father. He is waiting for us to give up the cheap things in our lives so that he can give us beautiful treasures.

God will never take away something without giving you something better in its place.

The Pickle Jar

The pickle jar as far back as I can remember sat on the floor beside the dresser in my parents' bedroom.

When he got ready for bed, Dad would empty his pockets and toss his coins into the jar. As a small boy, I was always fascinated at the sounds the coins made as they were dropped into the jar.

They landed with a merry jingle when the jar was almost empty. Then the tones gradually muted to a dull thud as the jar slowly filled.

I used to squat on the floor in front of the jar to admire the copper and silver circles that glinted like a pirate's treasure when the sun poured through the bedroom window.

When the jar was filled, Dad would sit at the kitchen table and roll the coins before taking them to the bank.

Taking the coins to the bank was always a big production.

Stacked neatly in a small cardboard box, the coins were placed between Dad and me on the seat of his old truck.

Each and every time, as we drove to the bank, Dad would look at me hopefully. 'Those coins are going to keep you out of the textile mill, son. You're going to do better than me. This old mill town's not going to hold you back.'

Also, each and every time, as he slid the box of rolled coins across the counter at the bank toward the cashier, he would grin proudly. 'These are for my son's college fund. He'll never work at the mill all his life like me.'

We would always celebrate each deposit by stopping for an ice cream cone. I always got chocolate. Dad always got vanilla. When the clerk at the ice cream parlor handed Dad his change, he would show me the few coins nestled in his palm.

When we got home, he started filling the jar again.

He always let me drop the first coins into the empty jar. As they rattled around with a brief, happy jingle, we grinned at each other.

'You'll get to college on pennies, nickels, dimes and quarters,' he said. 'But you'll get there; I'll see to that."

No matter how rough things got at home, Dad continued to doggedly drop his coins into the jar. Even the summer when Dad got laid off from the mill, and Mama had to serve dried beans several times a week, not a single dime was taken from the jar.

To the contrary, as Dad looked across the table at me, pouring catsup over my beans to make them more palatable, he became more determined than ever to make a way out for me, "When you finish college, Son," he told me, his eyes glistening, "You'll never have to eat beans again - unless you want to."

The years passed, and I finished college and took a job in another town. Once, while visiting my parents, I used the phone in their bedroom, and noticed that the pickle jar was gone. It had served its purpose and had been removed.

A lump rose in my throat as I stared at the spot beside the dresser where the jar had always stood. My dad was a man of few words: he never lectured me on the values of determination, perseverance, and faith. The pickle jar had taught me all these virtues far more eloquently than the most flowery of words could have done.

When I married, I told my wife Susan about the significant part the lowly pickle jar had played in my life as a boy. In my mind, it defined, more than anything else, how much my dad had loved me.

The first Christmas after our daughter Jessica was born, we spent the holiday with my parents. After dinner, Mom and Dad sat next to each other on the sofa, taking turns cuddling their first grandchild. Jessica began to whimper softly, and Susan took her from Dad's arms. 'She probably needs to be changed,' she said, carrying the baby into my parents' bedroom to diaper her. When Susan came back into the living room, there was a strange mist in her eyes.

She handed Jessica back to Dad before taking my hand and leading me into the room. "Look," she said softly, her eyes directing me to a spot on the floor beside the dresser. To my amazement, there, as if it had never been removed, stood the old pickle jar, the bottom already covered with coins. I walked over to the pickle jar, dug down into my pocket, and pulled out a fistful of coins. With a gamut of emotions choking me, I dropped the coins into the jar. I looked up and saw that Dad, carrying Jessica, had slipped quietly into the room. Our eyes locked, and I knew he was feeling the same emotions I felt. Neither one of us could speak. This truly touched my heart.

Sometimes we are so busy adding up our troubles that we forget to count our blessings. Never underestimate the power of your actions. With one small gesture you can change a person's life, for better or for worse. God puts us all in each other's lives to impact one another in some way. Look for GOOD in others.

The Storm

A pastor had been on a long flight between church conferences. The first warning of the approaching problems came when the sign on the airplane flashed on: Fasten Your Seat-Belts. Then, after a while, a calm voice said, "We shall not be serving the beverages at this time as we are expecting a little turbulence. Please be sure your seat belt is fastened."

As the pastor looked around the aircraft, it became obvious that many of the passengers were becoming apprehensive.

Later, the voice on the intercom said, "We are so sorry that we are unable to serve the meal at this time. The turbulence is still ahead of us."

And then the storm broke.

The ominous cracks of thunder could be heard even above the roar of the engines. Lightning lit up the darkening skies, and within moments that great plane was like a cork tossed around on a celestial ocean. One moment the airplane was lifted on terrific currents of air; the next, it dropped as if it were about to crash.

The pastor confessed that he shared the discomfort and fear of those around him. He said, "As I looked around the plane, I could see that nearly all the passengers were upset and alarmed. Some were praying. The future seemed ominous and many were wondering if they would make it through the storm."

"Then, I suddenly saw a little girl. Apparently the storm meant nothing to her. She had tucked her feet beneath her as she sat on her seat; she was reading a book and everything within her small world was calm and orderly. Sometimes she closed her eyes, then she would read again; then she would straighten her legs, but worry and fear were not in her world.

When the plane was being buffeted by the terrible storm when it lurched this way and that, as it rose and fell with frightening severity, when all the adults were scared half to death, that marvelous child was completely composed and unafraid."

The minister could hardly believe his eyes.

It was not surprising therefore, that when the plane finally reached its destination and all the passengers were hurrying to disembark, our pastor lingered to speak to the girl whom he had watched for such a long time.

Having commented about the storm and the behavior of the plane, he asked why she had not been afraid. The child replied,

"Cause my Daddy's the pilot, and he's taking me home."

There are many kinds of storms that buffet us. Physical, mental, financial, domestic, and many other storms can easily and quickly darken our skies and throw our plane into apparently uncontrollable movement. We have all known such times, and let us be honest and confess, it is much easier to be at rest when our feet are on the ground than when we are being tossed about a darkened sky.

Let us remember: Our Father is the Pilot.

He is in control and taking us home.

The Story of the Praying Hands

Back in the fifteenth century, in a tiny village near Nuremberg, lived a family with eighteen children. Eighteen! In order merely to keep food on the table for this mob, the father and head of the household, a goldsmith by profession, worked almost eighteen hours a day at his trade and any other paying chore he could find in the neighborhood.

Despite their seemingly hopeless condition, two of Albrecht Durer the Elder's children had a dream. They both wanted to pursue their talent for art, but they knew full well that their father would never be financially able to send either of them to Nuremberg to study at the Academy.

After many long discussions at night in their crowded bed, the two boys finally worked out a pact. They would toss a coin. The loser would go down into the nearby mines and, with his earnings, support his brother while he attended the academy. Then, when that brother who won the toss completed his studies, in four years, he would support the other brother at the academy, either with sales of his artwork or, if necessary, also by laboring in the mines. They tossed a coin on a Sunday morning after church. Albrecht Durer won the toss and went off to Nuremberg.

Albert went down into the dangerous mines and, for the next four years, financed his brother, whose work at the academy was almost an immediate sensation. Albrecht's etchings, his woodcuts, and his oils were far better than those of most of his professors, and by the time he graduated, he was beginning to earn considerable fees for his commissioned works.

When the young artist returned to his village, the Durer family held a festive dinner on their lawn to celebrate Albrecht's triumphant homecoming. After a long and memorable meal, punctuated with music and laughter, Albrecht rose from his honored position at the head of the table to drink a toast to his beloved brother for the years of sacrifice that had enabled Albrecht to fulfill his ambition. His closing words were, "And now, Albert, blessed brother of mine, now it is your turn. Now you can go to Nuremberg to pursue your dream, and I will take care of you."

All heads turned in eager expectation to the far end of the table where Albert sat, tears streaming down his pale face, shaking his lowered head from side to side while he sobbed and repeated, over and over, "No. No. No. No."

Finally, Albert rose and wiped the tears from his cheeks. He glanced down the long table at the faces he loved, and then, holding his hands close to his right cheek, he said softly, "No, brother. I cannot go to Nuremberg. It is too late for me. Look . . . look what four years in the mines have done to my hands! The bones in every finger have been smashed at least once, and lately I have been suffering from arthritis so badly in my right hand that I cannot even hold a glass to return your toast, much less make delicate lines on parchment or canvas with a pen or a brush. No, brother . . . for me it is too late."

More than 450 years have passed. By now, Albrecht Durer's hundreds of masterful portraits, pen and silver-point sketches, watercolors, charcoals, woodcuts, and copper engravings hang in every great museum in the world, but the odds are great that you, like most people, are familiar with only one of Albrecht Durer's works. More than merely being familiar with it, you very well may have a reproduction hanging in your home or office.

One day, to pay homage to Albert for all that he had sacrificed, Albrecht Durer painstakingly drew his brother's abused hands with palms together and thin fingers stretched skyward. He called his powerful drawing simply "Hands," but the entire world almost immediately opened their hearts to his great masterpiece and renamed his tribute of love "The Praying Hands."

The next time you see a copy of that touching creation, take a second look. Let it be your reminder, if you still need one, that no one – no one - ever makes it alone!

– *Author Unknown*

The Tablecloth

The brand new pastor and his wife, newly assigned to their first ministry, to reopen a church in suburban Brooklyn, arrived in early October excited about their opportunities. When they saw their church, it was very run down and needed much work. They set a goal to have everything done in time to have their first service on Christmas Eve.

They worked hard, repairing pews, plastering walls, painting, etc, and on December 18 were ahead of schedule and just about finished. On December 19 a terrible tempest - a driving rainstorm hit the area and lasted for two days.

On the 21st, the pastor went over to the church. His heart sank when he saw that the roof had leaked, causing a large area of plaster about 20 feet by 8 feet to fall off the front wall of the sanctuary just behind the pulpit, beginning about head high.

The pastor cleaned up the mess on the floor, and not knowing what else to do but postpone the Christmas Eve service, headed home.

On the way he noticed that a local business was having a flea market type sale for charity, so he stopped in. One of the items was a beautiful, handmade, ivory colored, crocheted tablecloth with exquisite work, fine colors and a Cross embroidered right in the center. It was just the right size to cover the hole in the front wall. He bought it and headed back to the church.

By this time it had started to snow. An older woman running from the opposite direction was trying to catch the bus. She missed it. The pastor invited her to wait in the warm church for the next bus 45 minutes later.

She sat in a pew and paid no attention to the pastor while he got a ladder, hangers, etc, to put up the tablecloth as a wall tapestry. The pastor could hardly believe how beautiful it looked and it covered up the entire problem area.

Then he noticed the woman walking down the center aisle. Her face was like a sheet. "Pastor," she asked, "where did you get that tablecloth?" The pastor explained.

The woman asked him to check the lower right corner to see if the initials, EBG were crocheted into it there. They were. These were the initials of the woman, and she had made this tablecloth 35 years before, in Austria.

The woman could hardly believe it as the pastor told how he had just gotten "The Tablecloth". The woman explained that before the war she and her husband were well-to-do people in Austria . When the Nazis came, she was forced to leave. Her husband was going to follow her the next week. He was captured, sent to prison and she never saw her husband or her home again.

The pastor wanted to give her the tablecloth; but she made the pastor keep it for the church. The pastor insisted on driving her home. That was the least he could do. She lived on the other side of Staten Island and was only in Brooklyn for the day for a housecleaning job

What a wonderful service they had on Christmas Eve. The church was almost full. The music and the spirit were great. At the end of the service, the pastor and his wife greeted everyone at the door and many said that they would return.

One older man, whom the pastor recognized from the neighborhood continued to sit in one of the pews and stare, and the pastor wondered why he wasn't leaving.

The man asked him where he got the tablecloth on the front wall because it was identical to one that his wife had made years ago when they lived in Austria before the war and how could there be two tablecloths so much alike?

He told the pastor how the Nazis came, how he forced his wife to flee for her safety and he was supposed to follow her, but he was arrested and put in a prison. He never saw his wife or his home again all the 35 years between.

The pastor asked him if he would allow him to take him for a little ride. They drove to Staten Island and to the same house where the pastor had taken the woman three days earlier. He helped the man climb the three flights of stairs to the woman's apartment, knocked on the door and he saw the greatest Christmas reunion he could ever imagine.

True Story - submitted by Pastor Rob Reid who says God does work in mysterious ways.

They Were Mine Before

There was a blind girl who hated herself because she was blind.

She hated everyone, except her loving boyfriend. He was always there for her. She told her boyfriend, "If I could only see the world, I would marry you."

One day, someone donated a pair of eyes to her.

When the bandages came off, she was able to see everything, including her boyfriend.

He asked her, "Now that you can see the world, will you marry me?"

The girl looked at her boyfriend and saw that he was blind.

The sight of his closed eyelids shocked her. She hadn't expected that. The thought of looking at them the rest of her life led her to refuse to marry him.

Her boyfriend left her in tears and days later wrote a note to her saying: 'Take good care of your eyes, my dear, for before they were yours, they were mine.'

This is how the human brain often works when our status changes.

Only a very few remember what life was like before, and who was always by their side in the most painful situations.

Today before you say an unkind word - Think of someone who can't speak.

Before you complain about the taste of your food, think of someone who has nothing to eat.

Before you complain about your husband or wife, think of someone who's crying out to GOD for a companion.

Today before you complain about life, think of someone who went too early to heaven.

Before you complain about your children, think of someone who desires children but they're barren.

Before you argue about your dirty house someone didn't clean or sweep, think of the people who are living in the streets.

Before whining about the distance you drive, think of someone who walks the same distance with their feet.

And when you are tired and complain about your job, think of the unemployed, the disabled, and those who wish they had your job.

But before you think of pointing the finger or condemning another, remember that not one of us is without sin and we all answer to one MAKER.

And when depressing thoughts seem to get you down, put a smile on your face and thank GOD you're alive and still around.

– Francis Shipp

Todd Beamer – Let's Roll

The week before September 11, 2001, America's "Tuesday of Terror," 32-year-old Todd Beamer and his wife, Lisa, had spent a romantic getaway in Italy. The couple, both 1991 graduates of Wheaton College, returned home Monday rested and relieved to be reunited with their boys David, 3, and Andrew, 1.

But extended family time would have to wait. The next morning Todd, an executive with Oracle, had to be at a sales reps meeting in Northern California. He kissed Lisa. who was five months pregnant with their third child, good-bye and headed to the Newark, New Jersey, airport, where he boarded United Flight 93 for San Francisco.

About 90 minutes into the westbound flight, the Boeing 757 was approaching Cleveland when three hijackers onboard identified themselves to the 34 passengers and 7 crew and proceeded to take control of the cockpit and cabin. The plane, now piloted by the would-be terrorists, made a sharp turn to the south.

Todd reached for the GTE Airfone in the back of one of the seats and was connected to a GTE supervisor on the ground. He explained to her what was happening and indicated that he and the other passengers would not likely survive. He presumed the pilot and copilot were already seriously injured or dead.

The GTE employee explained to Todd what had already happened at the World Trade Center and Pentagon. Upon hearing this news, Todd must have realized that the hijackers were intent on crashing the plane into another prominent building near Washington D.C. (the direction they were now headed). Even though the hijacker nearest Todd had a bomb belted around his middle, the former Wheaton College baseball player told the GTE representative that he and a few others were determined to do whatever they could to disrupt the terrorists' plan.

He then asked the person on the other end of the phone to call his wife and report their entire conversation to her (including how much he loved her). Before hanging up, this committed Christian and devoted family man, who taught Sunday school each week, asked the GTE employee to pray the Lord's Prayer with him. With the sound of passengers screaming in the background, she complied. When they concluded the prayer, Todd calmly said, "Help me, God. Help me, Jesus."

The GTE employee then heard Todd say, apparently to the other three businessmen he'd alluded to earlier: "Are you ready, guys? Let's roll!" With that the phone went dead.

Within a few minutes, Flight 93 was nose-diving into a rural field 80 miles southeast of Pittsburgh, where it left a crater 40 feet deep as it disintegrated upon impact. Because Todd Beamer was committed to Jesus Christ and his kingdom, he was willing to do whatever was necessary to put the needs of others above his own fear of danger and imminent death. Thanks to him and the three other businessmen who joined with him, the intended target in the nation's capital was not reached, and who knows how many lives were saved because of that. No one on the ground was killed.

According to Todd's wife, Lisa, "His example of courage has given me, my boys (and my unborn baby) a reason to live."

That's what can happen when we, like Jesus Christ, put the needs of others ahead of our own.

Unconditional Acceptance

I am a mother of three (ages 14, 12, 3) and have recently completed my college degree. The last class I had to take was Sociology. The teacher was absolutely inspiring with the qualities that I wish every human being had been graced with. Her last project of the term was called "Smile." The class was asked to go out and smile at three people and document their reactions. I am a very friendly person and always smile at everyone and say hello anyway, so, I thought this would be a piece of cake, literally.

Soon after we were assigned the project, my husband, youngest son, and I went out to McDonald's one crisp March morning. It was just our way of sharing special play time with our son. We were standing in line, waiting to be served, when all of a sudden everyone around us began to back away, and then even my husband did. I did not move an inch... an overwhelming feeling of panic welled up inside of me as I turned to see why they had moved.

As I turned around I smelled a horrible "dirty body" smell, and there standing behind me were two poor homeless men. As I looked down at the short gentleman, close to me, he was "smiling." His beautiful sky blue eyes were full of God's Light as he searched for acceptance. He said, "Good day" as he counted the few coins he had been clutching. The second man fumbled with his hands as he stood behind his friend. I realized the second man was mentally deficient and the blue eyed gentleman was his salvation. I held my tears as I stood there with them. The young lady at the counter asked him what they wanted. He said, "Coffee is all Miss" because that was all they could afford. (If they wanted to sit in the restaurant and warm up, they had to buy something. He just wanted to be warm). Then I really felt it-the compulsion was so great I almost reached out and embraced the little man with the blue eyes.

That is when I noticed all eyes in the restaurant were set on me, judging my every action. I smiled and asked the young lady behind the counter to give me two more breakfast meals on a separate tray. I then walked around the corner to the table that the men had chosen as a resting spot. I put the tray on the table and laid my hand on the blue eyed gentleman's cold hand.

He looked up at me, with tears in his eyes, and said, "Thank you." I leaned over, began to pat his hand and said, "I did not do this for you. God is here working through me to give you hope." I started to cry as I walked away to join my husband and son.

When I sat down my husband smiled at me and said, "That is why God gave you to me, Honey. To give me hope." We held hands for a moment and at that time we knew that only because of the Grace that we had been given were we able to give.

That day showed me the pure Light of God's sweet love. I returned to college, on the last evening of class, with this story in hand. I turned in "My Project" and the instructor read it. Then she looked up at me and said, "Can I share this?" I slowly nodded as she got the attention of the class.

She began to read and that is when I knew that we as human beings and being part of God, share this need to heal people and be healed. In my own way I had touched the people at McDonald's, my husband, son, instructor, and every soul that shared the classroom on the last night I spent as a college student.

I graduated with one of the biggest lessons I would ever learn:

UNCONDITIONAL ACCEPTANCE.

Much love and compassion is to each and every person who may read this and learn how to LOVE PEOPLE AND USE THINGS - NOT LOVE THINGS AND USE PEOPLE.

– *Author Unknown*

When You Thought I Wasn't Looking

A message every adult should read because children are watching you and doing as you do, not as you say.

When you thought I wasn't looking I saw you hang my first painting on the refrigerator, and I immediately wanted to paint another one.

When you thought I wasn't looking I saw you feed a stray cat, and I learned that it was good to be kind to animals.

When you thought I wasn't looking I saw you make my favorite cake for me, and I learned that the little things can be the special things in life.

When you thought I wasn't looking I heard you say a prayer, and I knew that there is a God I could always talk to, and I learned to trust in Him.

When you thought I wasn't looking I saw you make a meal and take it to a friend who was sick, and I learned that we all have to help take care of each other.

When you thought I wasn't looking I saw you take care of our house and everyone in it, and I learned we have to take care of what we are given.

When you thought I wasn't looking I saw how you handled your responsibilities, even when you didn't feel good, and I learned that I would have to be responsible when I grow up.

When you thought I wasn't looking I saw tears come from your eyes, and I learned that sometimes things hurt, but it's all right to cry.

When you thought I wasn't looking I saw that you cared, and I wanted to be everything that I could be.

When you thought I wasn't looking I learned most of life's lessons that I need to know to be a good and productive person when I grow up.

When you thought I wasn't looking I looked at you and wanted to say,' Thanks for all the things I saw when you thought I wasn't looking.'

Each of us (parent, grandparent, aunt, uncle, teacher, friend) influences the life of a child.

How will you touch the life of someone today?

Live simply. Love generously. Care deeply. Speak kindly.

Whoever Takes the Son Gets it All

A wealthy man and his son loved to collect rare works of art. They had everything in their collection, from Picasso to Raphael. They would often sit together and admire the great works of art.

When the Vietnam conflict broke out, the son went to war. He was very courageous and died in battle while rescuing another soldier. The father was notified and grieved deeply for his only son.

About a month later, just before Christmas, there was a knock at the door. A young man stood at the door with a large package in his hands. He said, "Sir, you don't know me, but I am the soldier for whom your son gave his life. He saved many lives that day, and he was carrying me to safety when a bullet struck him in the heart and he died instantly. He often talked about you, and your love for art."

The young man held out this package. "I know this isn't much. I'm not really a great artist, but I think your son would have wanted you to have this."

The father opened the package. It was a portrait of his son, painted by the young man. He stared in awe at the way the soldier had captured the personality of his son in the painting. The father was so drawn to the eyes that his own eyes welled up with tears.

He thanked the young man and offered to pay him for the picture. "Oh, no sir, I could never repay what your son did for me. It's a gift."

The father hung the portrait over his mantle. Every time visitors came to his home he took them to see the portrait of his son before he showed them any of the other great works he had collected.

The man died a few months later. There was to be a great auction of his paintings. Many influential people gathered, excited over seeing the great paintings and having an opportunity to purchase one for their collection.

On the platform sat the painting of the son. The auctioneer pounded his gavel. "We will start the bidding with this picture of the son. Who will bid for this picture?" There was silence.

Then a voice in the back of the room shouted, "We want to see the famous paintings. Skip this one."

But the auctioneer persisted. "Will somebody bid for this painting. Who will start the bidding? $100, $200?" Another voice angrily."We didn't come to see this painting. We came to see the Van Goghs, the Rembrandt's. Get on with the real bids!"

But still the auctioneer continued. "The son! The son! Who'll take the son?"

Finally, a voice came from the very back of the room. It was the longtime gardener of the man and his son. "I'll give $10 for the painting." Being a poor man, it was all he could afford.

"We have $10, who will bid $20?"

"Give it to him for $10. Let's see the masters."

"$10 is the bid, won't someone bid $20?"

The crowd was becoming angry. They didn't want the picture of the son. They wanted the more worthy investments for their collections.

The auctioneer pounded the gavel. "Going once, twice, SOLD for $10!"

A man sitting on the second row shouted, "Now let's get on with the collection!"

The auctioneer laid down his gavel. "I'm sorry, the auction is over"

"What about the paintings?"

"I am sorry. When I was called to conduct this auction, I was told of a secret stipulation in the will. I was not allowed to reveal that stipulation until this time. Only the painting of the son would be auctioned. Whoever bought that painting would inherit the entire estate, including the paintings. The man who took the son gets everything!"

God gave His son 2,000 years ago to die on the cross. Much like the auctioneer, His message today is: "The son, the son, who'll take the son?" Because, you see, whoever takes the Son gets everything.

FOR GOD SO LOVED THE WORLD HE GAVE HIS ONLY BEGOTTEN SON, WHO SO EVER BELIEVETH, SHALL HAVE ETERNAL LIFE. THAT'S LOVE

– *Author Unknown*

Other Books by Glen Wheeler

All books are available from your local bookstore, Amazon, Barnes and Noble, Legacy, and Koinonia Associates.

A Funny Thing Happened on My Way to the Retirement Home.

Published 2011 Price: $13.95

140 pages of humor for and about Senior Citizens will bring the reader many smiles and hearty laughter. Gleaned from his many years as a minister and as a chaplain to the residents of a retirement home, this book will affirm that Seniors indeed have "the time of their lives." All Seniors have their fears and worries, but leaving their homes for a retirement center is a deeply emotional experience. These humorous stories will bring smiles to their faces.

Bedpan Devotions
– Reflections on Recovering from an Extended Illness.

Published 2010 Price: $12.95

Excellent counsel for those with long term home confinement, cancer, heart problems, broken bones, and similar illnesses. Written while recovering from a broken hip, the author deals with the various emotions experienced throughout a long illness—fear, bills, loneliness, blood draws, visitors, food, medicines, faith and prayers. This is an excellent gift to give when you visit or send to a loved one or friend in a distant city.

Widowers Hurt, Too.

Published 2009 Price: $12.95

Materials to encourage a widower are very limited. After his wife passed away, the author found that the adjustments were far greater than he ever imagined. Seeking helpful material, he found very little. He relates how he faced the challenges of loneliness, eating along, decision making, retiring alone, the empty pew at church, considering having a date, and many, many others. The book is excellent for widows, too, in spite of its title. His lengthy ministerial experiences are reflected in the relating of his personal journey. He suggests waiting to give the book 3-4 weeks after the spouse's passing.

The author may be contacted at: Glen Wheeler
165 Highbluffs Blvd. # 413
Columbus, OH 43235

About the Author

Having lived in a retirement village since 1989, and after twelve years as the chaplain, I decided that my retirement ministry would be writing books for Seniors. My goal is to produce a book each year. I believe I can say, "Have been there and done that!"

This is book # 4. From my files, I have selected articles which are inspiring, informative, and contain worthwhile material. If you know a Senior with limitations, a handicapped youth, young adult or Adult, these articles are worth reading to them. Take time to do so.

I graduated from Lincoln High School, Vincennes, IN in 1943 and from Johnson Bible College (now Johnson University,) Knoxville, TN. in 1947. In 1944 I was ordained to the Christian ministry and what a marvelous journey it has been.

I am grateful the Lord let me labor in His vineyard.

Glen Wheeler- Columbus, OH.